BREAK THE RULES

BREAK
the RULES

An Uncommon Guide to Creating the Life You Crave

Sylvia Theisen

Requests for permission to make any kind of copies of any part of
the book should be made in writing and submitted to: Sylvia Theisen,
700 Colorado Boulevard, Suite 343, Denver, CO 80206, USA.
www.sylviatheisen.com

Cover design by Paul Vorreiter
Interior design by Michelle M. White
Editor: Alexandra O'Connell

To my Mom, Vera Castelli Theisen –
who has always been a woman ahead of her time.
I appreciate that you have never seen limitations
in what is possible, and for the incredible way you
have modeled that by your own life choices.

Contents

Introduction

How many people do you know well who are incredibly happy and fulfilled in their life? I'm talking about genuinely happy, not the superficial Facebook version sporting family photos with matching navy blue shirts and perfect smiles. People who are living fulfilled lives on a deeper level: their family life is easy, they are in great physical health, their personal relationships are vibrant, they are thriving financially, free from addictions, they are living in alignment with their values. Think about it for a moment. What number do you come up with?

When I ask that same question at my live events, people think hard before identifying 0-2 people whom they know well and can confidently say they seem to be enjoying a full and wonderful life. With so many people being unhappy, then, where did we get the idea that following what everyone else is doing is the formula for creating our best life?

If you want to create a fulfilling life, it is going to require that you do some things differently than most everyone you know.

Shaking it Up

You're looking for something different. I know that because for whatever reason you picked up this book. You may be wondering, "Is this all there is?" You may be going through a major life crisis that has you questioning the way you've always done things and the choices you've made so far. You may be a life-long lover of self-improvement programs but after doing a lot of personal growth work, you still find you're not experiencing enough of the life you crave. Or, things may be going pretty well but there is one area in your life that you know you'd like to see some changes. In any case, here you are. I'm going to show you some simple but powerful ways to get on a path of creating more of what you want—and less of what you don't.

As you begin to try some new things and leave your old ways behind, you are likely to get comments from those who know you well. They may ask why you are not your "old self." They may try to guilt or shame you into doing things the way you've always done them in the past. Remind yourself that it takes courage to veer off the well-worn path and forge ahead to decide for yourself whether you like the results you are getting. Adopting new habits may feel awkward and not like your usual self. As the saying goes, "If you always do what you've always done, you always get what you've always gotten." What we want is change, not the same old thing.

After counseling hundreds of people in my psychotherapy practice, I've learned what contributes to people feeling fatigued, burned out and depressed. I've also learned what makes them wake up excited about their life, and creating work, relationships and fun that fuels them in every way. These ideas are field-tested. Everything I will outline has been tested by hundreds of others. The results are in—it works!

In addition to my professional expertise as a psychotherapist, I've also read self-help and personal development books my whole life. My bookshelves are filled from decades of reading similar genre books. I noticed that one of the common themes in online reviews of self-help books is the reader expressing disappointment in that it didn't offer "something new". We are always looking for something new, preferably earth shattering, quick and effortless. Even better if it's free and wrapped in chocolate. The reality is that there is no magic pill or quick fix. Un-learning the fundamental rules by which you've created your life may seem too basic and yet it is has the potential to be life changing. When you change the foundation upon which you build everything else, any area of your life can shift for the better. Typically, people try to make big changes on the outside (new partners, new careers, new health goals, new income levels) without changing anything on the inside and then wonder why they are frustrated and lacking results. We rarely have the time, opportunity or inclination to take a good look at what beliefs we've been living by, let alone uncovering them and finding ways to change them. My hope is that some of these rules will resonate with you and that you practice the suggested activities for change. In doing so, I know you can experience massive positive change. I use the word "practice' intentionally. The value in any personal development is not to just read it, but to apply the material and use it over a period of time. A year ago, my sister and I made a pact to do yoga three times a week to improve our posture. Months into it, one of the yoga instructors gave me some encouragement at the end of a class, after seeing that I was finding it challenging. When I bemoaned my disappointment that despite doing yoga for months, I wasn't feeling the difference, she smiled and said " That's why we call it a practice". She went on to talk about how it is a life long practice, not a quick remedy.

You may not need to make a radical change in your life and uproot anything (although you may choose to). You will, however need to be willing to dismantle the rules you've held as unquestionable truths. I'm going to shine the light on twelve of the most common beliefs that people are operating by, and that don't tend to work well. They are ones that are so familiar, you may not even question whether they are habits. Hey, everyone else is doing them too! But they are keeping you chained to your dissatisfaction.

It takes courage to look at ourselves and try new behaviors and ways of thinking. It's so much easier to keep doing it the way we've always done it. More so than anything another book, workshop or self-help guru can tell you—trust your own inner guidance more than anyone else's. You already know the answers if you get quiet and listen to yourself. What I'll share in this book are tools and ideas about changing habits that are getting in your own way. The way our society is set up today gives so much credence to outside influences, whether it is social media reminding us of how everyone else's life looks more exciting, movies that want us to believe we could have a Hollywood style marriage, or commercials and retailers convincing us we'll be happy when we have one more new thing. There is little in place to remind you that you are wiser than you give yourself credit for and that you know best. The truth is, no one knows what will make you happy better than you do. This book gives you a road map to look at each belief and determine whether it is working in your life or limiting you and the life you crave. Ultimately, only you can decide what you need to let go of, what you need to think differently about and what you're willing to try that is new and unfamiliar.

Years ago, I read this and stuck it in one of my journals. I have since read it dozens of times. It identifies some of the reasons we don't go for what we really want in life and how it is often our guilt or fear that are the biggest obstacles.

> Your ultimate goal in life is to become your best self. Your immediate goal is to get on the path that will lead you there. Why should you feel guilty if you refuse to be intimidated by someone who persists in

standing in the way of your being that best self or who is "hurt" when you finally manage it?

The highest love a person can have for you is to wish for you to evolve into the best person you can be. No one owns you, no matter what your relationship. You are not here on this earth to fulfill the unmet dreams of a frustrated parent or to protect another person from the reality of himself in the world.

You are here to develop and grow, to do your share to make the outside world a better place to live, to make the immediate place in which you live, the world that is you, as honest and as true to your feelings as you possibly can.

– Author Unknown

Let's get started!

BREAK THE RULES

Breaking Rules and Courage

"It is easier to sail many thousands of miles
through cold and storm and cannibals, in a
government ship, with five hundred men and boys
to assist one, than it is to explore the private sea, the
Atlantic and Pacific ocean of one's being alone."

– Henry David Theoreau

None of us were given a guidebook on how to create our life. The easiest thing to do is to look around and observe what everyone else seems to be doing as some sort of GPS. Go to school, get a job, find a partner, maybe have some kids, buy a house, hate your boss, get a different job, have a midlife crisis, get fat and complain about it, take some cool trips if you can afford it, spend your weekend watching grown men running around with a ball and yell your brains out at them so you have something to talk about at the office on Monday morning, eventually start complaining about how your body is failing you and everything hurts, start thinking about retirement, end up in a nursing home drooling on yourself, you know...the usual.

Funny thing about us humans, we tend to get suspicious of people who aren't following the crowd. Someone decides not to have children, or quits their soul crushing corporate job and we hear hushed tones of concern about the one who is breaking away from the pack. "Is everything ok?" people ask—as if there is some mental instability in thinking independently.

In the end, you are the only one who will decide whether you feel good about the way you have lived your life. This point became painfully clear to me when in 2005, my husband, Garry, was diagnosed with late stage kidney cancer. After a five-month battle including emergency surgery and chemotherapy, he passed away at the age of fifty-five. Sitting at his bedside in his final hours, I was struck by how death is a solo sport. We spend much of our lives worrying about what others think of us. We wrench our hands and hearts about how our choices will look to others and how it might impact them. Yet, the reality is, no friend or family is going to leave the planet with us and ride along to assure us that we've done well. Furthermore, no one is actually going to think much about our choices after we've gone let alone give a crap. It sounds harsh, but it's true. We certainly miss people who have left us. But it's unlikely we spend a lot of time reviewing their lives other than how they affected us. Despite all our goodness, we are a self-absorbed species.

As a first step, it might behoove you to quit assuming that other people are watching you, thinking about you, and judging you. They're generally not. Instead, look internally, rather than externally for direction. The biggest changes in life happen when you begin to look inward and trust yourself for guidance. As you develop this new habit, you'll likely find you need to break some rules. This book will urge you to dig deep and find the courage to forge your own path. It will encourage you to do what feels un-natural. Do you remember the classic optical illusions? The black and white image looks like an old woman with a big nose until you look more deeply at it and finally, you see that there is also a beautiful young woman. Once you see the young woman, you can then go back and forth between the two images. Well, life is much the same. You'll begin to see yourself and your life in a new way so that you can make new choices and weave between the old and the new.

Before we talk about rules and breaking them, let's take a moment to look at our beliefs about risk and courage. After all, it takes some level of risk and courage to break the rules.

Challenge

In earlier eras, people were willing to brave extreme conditions to go after their dream life. Getting to the port nearest them was a big adventure in itself—traveling by foot, train, or on a mule's back. Once at port, they may have timed it right, or they may have found themselves waiting around for weeks or months until the next ship left. Finally on board, the trip took many days of traveling across the ocean, headed to Ellis Island in a crowded boat through severe weather, smelly passengers, and gross conditions. If you weren't physically ill and puking, most of the people around you were. Arriving with no job, no support system and very little money was just the beginning. All of this was endured to chase the dream of a better life.

Later in our history, people took great risks again during the gold rush. Inspired to go after fortunes, people were willing to travel for months on unknown roads, with limited supplies and only a vision of what might be possible. Losing loved ones who died on the trail, running out of food, and freezing to death all seemed worth it in order to have a chance at the good life.

These days, as a culture, we've become soft. Our local Starbucks barista being out of soy milk can send us over the edge. We whine about traffic while sitting in our car with heated leather seats for butt warmers; we complain about poor service while we're enjoying a luxury resort with unlimited food and poolside margaritas. We demand that our children have perfect school environments. What happened to our pioneer spirit? What are we willing to risk now for what we want? In comparison to past generations, it appears we are not willing to risk much of anything.

It is interesting that participation in extreme endurance events like Ironman triathlons has increased in record numbers in the past two decades. It seems we are more likely to challenge ourselves physically in a competitive situation even when it requires a substantial investment of time and money. Yet, how likely are we to push ourselves in day-to-day events? Could it be the monotony and safety of the life we've created is the very thing that pushes us in extreme ways in our spare time?

The question of risk-taking in today's culture struck me recently when I sold the house I'd lived in for fifteen years and moved to a different neighborhood just a few miles away, still within central Denver. During the course of the move, several people said to me, "You're so brave!" While I appreciated the sentiment, it struck me as an odd comment. Moving a few miles is a brave thing to do? I can appreciate that risk and our tolerance for change is a very individual thing and not for anyone else to judge. Yet, it did make me wonder if we've gotten too comfortable, accepting a very low bar for risk-taking.

At the same time in our culture, we seem to have become hung up on fear. Libraries, bookstores, and podcasts are filled with messages that encourage us to feel the fear and do it anyway, don't feed the fear, break through your fear, and other clichés. We've heard every version of these sayings many times. Fear is like any other emotion—it's going to surface, and it's going to pass. We all experience it on a regular basis. Just like we experience sadness, guilt, shame, joy, excitement, happiness, and a whole lot of other emotions. Do we say "feel the happiness, or break through your happiness"? No, we just enjoy it when it comes to us, knowing it will pass.

You are destined to live a small and boring life if your goal is to experience as little fear as possible. Because of that, I'm more concerned about when I don't feel fear than when I do. How small am I living? How safe have I made my life if nothing feels uncomfortable?

I've always liked Eleanor Roosevelt's quote: "Do one thing that scares you every day." She suggests that we can make a daily practice of feeling scared, just as we do with physical exercise, eating, and sleeping. Feeling fear can be as expected as the need to brush our teeth which seems to offer a healthier approach than trying to eliminate it.

It is likely that when you start to do things differently, there will be times that you'll fear you're headed in the wrong direction. That's a normal response to change. I love the following example from nature that simplifies the experience of turning around when we run into the unfamiliar.

The Wasp Trap

A wasp trap is a simple backyard device that attracts, traps, and kills wasps. It's an easy way to stop them from bothering you and your guests at an outdoor BBQ. You can buy one, or you can easily make one yourself by taking a soda bottle, putting some sweet liquid on the bottom, and turning it upside down. It is then ready to hang from a tree. But, before hanging it, you need to do one more thing. Take black duct tape and wrap it around the top third of the bottle and leave a small opening for the wasp to enter.

The wasp will be drawn to the sweetness and enter the trap. When it's ready to leave, it heads towards the bottom of the bottle. But, when it senses the darkness created by the duct tape, it feels like it's going the wrong way. It repeatedly flies back up to the light which keeps it enclosed and eventually kills it. The only way out of the bottle cone is to fly into the darkness. It's counterintuitive—the wasp feels as though it is going deeper into the bottle rather than escaping. In reality, what feels like the wrong direction is the only way out of the trap. Much like humans: we often turn around to return to our old ways too quickly instead of pushing through the uncertainty of the darkness initially experienced when trying something new.

Quit Hitting the Snooze Button

At a time when we have seemingly unlimited options, we've gotten comfortable taking the easy way. If that were creating a lot of happiness for you, you probably wouldn't be reading this book and being open to thinking about what could be different. Breaking a few rules is going to feel risky, uncomfortable, and at times, downright crazy. The alternative is to put down this book and keep doing things the way you've always done them and to keep getting similar results.

There is that book you're going to write. You're going to get in shape and finally take the extra weight off. You'll quit smoking, once and for all. Eventually, you know you'll make peace with your dad. All those things that we think we're going to eventually tackle, just not yet.

I've never found inspiration in the old saying, "Live as if today is the last day of your life." If that were true, I might lounge in my pajamas, eating sea salt chocolate with almonds and drinking pinot noir. Instead, I prefer "live as if you're leaving for the airport tonight." Now, that kicks my butt into gear. I get more done the day before I'm headed out on vacation than I usually get done in a month. I have my list and I'm checking things off like a crazy woman. It's amazing.

I cringe with the recent popularity of the "bucket list." If there are things you want to be doing, what about being present and doing them instead of either putting them off or putting them in a bucket? You hate your job? What are you doing about it? You feel like you're in a dead marriage but you're waiting until your kids graduate from high school because you don't want to disrupt their senior year? Oh wait, now they're out of college but you think you should wait because they're job hunting and it might throw them off their game.

Seriously?

One of the well-meaning but stupid things people say when someone dies is, "It's so sad they went before their time." Um, it was their time. That's why they're gone. Life doesn't owe us or guarantee a certain number of years. We're all going to die—no one is getting out of here alive. It is amazing how we stop hitting the snooze button for the things we really want. What are you waiting for?

You know that you are craving something different than what you currently have in your life. That quiet yearning that nudges you and says, "Is this all there is?" You've told the voice to go away, you've practiced being happy with what you have but underneath it all, you know you're snoozing.

Time to wake up.

You are Here

You'll get the most out of this book if you pause here to take a look at where you are now. Most of us are painfully aware of what we don't like about our life but that's only one view of a bigger picture. There are probably some things you are very pleased about, and positive attributes about yourself that you don't need to change. Is there one thing in particular that you are dissatisfied with and motivated to change or are you experiencing a general malaise in that nothing is really wrong yet nothing is great either? I offer these questions as a starting place for you to take a deep breath and tune in to how you see your life today. If, like me, you don't like making permanent personal notes in a book (because what if someone picks it up and reads our innermost thoughts?) , grab a sheet of paper and take the time to run through these. Jot down the first thing that pops into your mind, even if it sounds strange. Often times, our first and un-edited answer gives us the most interesting insight.

1. The area of my life that I feel most pleased with is:

_____

_____

_____

_____

2. When I think about what I need to change, I think about:

3. One belief that keeps me from having what I want is:

4. The qualities I most admire in myself are:

5. What makes me feel sad and regretful is:

6. In my ideal life, I would be:

7. If I had the courage, I would:

_____

_____

_____

8. If I needed to forgive myself for something, it would be:

_____

_____

_____

9. The person in my life who most supports me in reaching my fullest potential is:

_____

_____

_____

10. If I'm honest, I know I need to eliminate:

_____

_____

_____

While sometimes it's tough to take a totally honest look at ourselves and the choices we've made, it can also be motivating. The good news is that whatever you've created thus far can be changed and improved by making new choices. Every GPS route requires a starting point as well as an endpoint to guide us well. Use this as a starting point.

I have no sense of geographical direction. I don't mean that directions don't come naturally to me and so I don't take the front seat to navigate. I mean that when I get off an exit on the highway, I don't know which way I came from when I go to get back on. Walking out of a shopping mall (I'm actually allergic to shopping malls, but that's another story) I have no idea where my car is. Not, is it at Big Bear Lot 1 or Zebra Lot 2? But as in: "Did I even park in this lot at all?" I've learned to hide my handicap over the years, and as technology progressed, so did my methods. In the early days, I took notes of where I parked and the names of the street signs nearby. Eventually, I graduated to taking photos on my smartphone and eventually, hit the jackpot with GPS, which has radically changed my life. I love Siri telling me I'm being rerouted. To me, it's the equivalent of someone throwing me a rescue rope in cold water.

You have your own rescue rope, your own GPS route available to you. It will always tell you where you are. You are here. In your life. This life. Whatever you've created is in large part because of the choices you've made. You chose your education, your profession, your partner, your fitness level, your attitude, your friends, your hobby (or lack of) and the good news is that you can make different choices that will result in a different kind of life. Are you owning it? Own that even if your life seems terrible, you're in it. If you can't own that you are "here", it's going to make it harder to get "there".

Have you ever noticed how your mindset, self-esteem, and communication go with you? We can change jobs, partners, living situations, and yet we still see themes running through it all. Before you look to externals for ways to change your life, what might happen if you stay right where you are and take a closer look at the internals—your self-limiting beliefs, habits, and mindset?

Moving has been referred to as the geographical cure—the belief that a move to another home or another city will fix everything. The new-ness of the change may initially create some excitement and good energy. Before long, however, the dust settles and you realize that you have not addressed the underlying issues. We overestimate the impact our external circumstances have on us and we underestimate the power of the internal elements.

You can blame your childhood, your parents, your teachers, your boss, your size, your age, your health, your religion, the economy, the President of the United States, the Pope, your zodiac sign, but you and I know, it's you. You're it. You can keep complaining out loud about everything that is wrong but here's the deal—lean in close and I'll tell you the big secret: no one else is buying it. They actually think you're the problem too. They may be polite and hear you out, but inside they're thinking, "I'm so sick of hearing him complain about this," and if you keep doing what you're doing, you're going to be that person that acquaintances avoid when they see you in the grocery store. You thought you were going to say hello but next thing you know the person disappeared into the cat food aisle, not to be seen again.

While it may initially feel depressing to own that it is your choices that got you to this place, it can also be liberating. It can be an exciting eye opener to realize you can make different choices to create radically different results. On the other hand, if you keep believing that your current circumstances are all a result of other people and external events, there is not much you can do about that. As long as you stay focused on external reasons that your life has gone the way it has, you remain a victim to those very excuses.

Most people are, of course, also victims of the choices of others in significant ways. You may have been abused as a kid, you may have had a business partner screw you over and take all your money, you may have had a spouse who beat you or cheated on you. Maybe you were swept up in a financial crisis that caused devastation. Yes, these things happened. Now, you have control over how you choose to react to these events. We can choose to spend a lifetime on the pain and hurt of that abuse or we can choose to work through it, understand how it impacts us, and then decide what we want to focus on differently. A universal truth is that whatever you focus on will increase. Guaranteed. It will benefit you to choose what you want to focus on so that you are in control of choosing what you want more of.

Do people who come in contact with you leave your presence feeling uplifted, loved, appreciated? Or, do they feel drained after listening to your misery? If it's the latter, you can change that. Now. Immediately. In this moment, by the choices you make.

Maybe Yes, Maybe No

As you begin to question your long-standing interpretations of what has happened in your life and who has wronged you, it might be too big of a stretch to go from that prior stance to an attitude that everything is happening as it should and everyone is doing the best they can. If that's the case, a smaller step in the right direction is to move to a neutral position. Loosen your grip on all that seems unfair and see if you can keep an open mind to other possible viewpoints. This classic story helps with the process. See if you identify yourself more in the role of the villagers or the elderly man.

There was a village in which a person's wealth was determined by the number of horses they owned. There was a wise old man who was considered the wealthiest man in the land and who by far owned the most horses. One day, while the horses were playing in a fenced-in area, they got out through a hole in the fence. The horses galloped away and soon all the villagers heard of the epic event.

"Oh no, that's terrible!" they exclaimed as they showed up at the old man's land to offer support. The old man calmly shook his head and softly said, "Maybe yes, maybe no."

The next day the old man's workers found the lost horses and with them, they brought back a herd of wild horses. The news traveled quickly through town and again, the villagers had a strong reaction. "This is amazing!" they said. "How wonderful! You now have twice the number of horses you previously had and have doubled your wealth!" The old man said, "Maybe yes, maybe no."

Shortly thereafter, the man's son was out breaking in one of the wild horses when he was thrown off the horse and broke his leg. "Oh, how awful!" the villagers said. "We heard your son is injured and can't help you on the land."

"Maybe yes, maybe no."

The next day, the army came through to recruit all the able-bodied men of a certain age to go off to war. They were unable to take the son because of his injury. What at first seemed a disaster turned out to be a stroke of luck. The story continues in this vein, always presenting opportunities to react with judgment or to remain neutral. Maybe yes, maybe no.

Practice this. Practice holding off on making snap judgments about a situation until it further unfolds. Avoid being a drama queen (or king) and not making the worst possible scenario your default setting.

Things will change, one way or another. Often, it's worth waiting to see what's around the bend and like the wise man in the story, develop a "Maybe yes, maybe no" habit of reacting. What if, like the wise man, we first assumed that life is on our side and then waited to see what good was going to emerge from a situation? This seems a less stressful way to go through life than to imagine there is disaster around every corner.

Think about a time in your own life when you were sure something terrible was happening and it ended up having a real silver lining or didn't end up being as bad as you initially thought. I'm reminded of the quote that has many variations, by people from Mark Twain to Thomas Jefferson, and which says, in essence: "I've experienced a lot of terrible things. . . most of which have never happened."

My Dad is one of the big influences in my life and he was the first person who showed me how to be an optimist and a realist at the same time. Growing up, I repeatedly heard him say, "Look at the donut and not the hole," which as a teenager, I found incredibly annoying. As an adult it is a great reminder that there is always a choice about what we focus on. We don't need to deny reality but we also don't need to focus on lack and disaster.

What if everyone is doing the best they can (given who they are and their current circumstances)? It's easy to judge others and make up a story about why we think they are making the choices they are—personalizing it to be something about us, assuming they are angry or intentionally sabotaging us. What if everyone (including you!) are doing the very best they can with what they have to work with in the moment: the resources of time, energy, money, mindset, understanding, emotional maturity, and so on. That annoying driver who is on your tail in traffic? Maybe he just found out his spouse is in the hospital and is racing to get there. The critical co-worker who is minimizing your value and criticizing your project? Maybe they are debating whether they will need to file bankruptcy and feeling poorly about themselves, taking it out on you and others.

Try scripting your life as if everyone has shown up perfectly according to a plan for what you needed to learn in the moment. Ex-lovers, teachers, children—all put on earth to share the road with you.

Steve Jobs said it well when he said, "You can't connect the dots looking forward; you can only connect them looking backwards. So, you have to trust that the dots will somehow connect in your future. You have to trust in something—your gut, destiny, life, karma, whatever. Because believing that the dots will connect down the road will give you the confidence to follow your heart even when it leads you off the well-worn path; and that will make all the difference."

Assume that life is conspiring to give you what you want. Everyone and everything is on your side. If you are going to be suspicious, best to assume that all is slanted in your favor.

Likewise, I encourage you to read this book with a "maybe yes, maybe no" attitude. Rather than disregard something as not applicable to you, sit with it and be open minded. Often times, the things that irritate us most are the very ones we need to pay attention to.

RULE #1
Follow the Rules

RULE BREAKER
Don't Believe Everything You Believe

The very first rule you'll need to break is "follow the rules."

As adults, the rules of life may be unspoken and more vague than when we were children. Wash your hands, finish your dinner, do your homework, don't talk back to your parents were among the very clear rules that were ingrained in us. As adults, we tend to assume there are a lot of rules, when there are few. Don't lie, kill, or steal are a few that come to mind. In the first phase of examining this idea of breaking the rules, you may need to argue with yourself about whether, in fact, this is a rule you believe in or one you adopted after hearing so often and then never questioned. For the purpose of this book, the word "rule" is used interchangeably with any long held belief that you live by as if it is truth.

You're going to have to loosen your grip on the way you've always known things to be. You have heard some of these rules hundreds, if not thousands of times, and some of them may be so ingrained in you that it is tough to even recognize that they are not truths, they are beliefs.

I mentioned earlier that I recently sold my home of fifteen years. The home where I walked my son Tanner to his first day of kindergarten and also packed him up for college. The home where I laid in bed with my husband for the last time before the ambulance transported him to hospice. The home where I met my running buddy (I would have missed so many 6 a.m. runs if Lisa hadn't been waiting patiently on my porch for me), made lifetime friends, and experienced plenty of seasons of laughing and crying. Inevitably, when someone heard I was moving, their response was, "Moving sucks," or "Oh, you must be stressed."

No. I didn't experience a single moment of stress during the move. Was it a lot of work? Yes. Did it create some temporary chaos? Absolutely. Was it stressful? Not once.

Before I'd even packed the first set of wine glasses in bubble wrap, I had decided that I was going to enjoy the entire process. I took my time and enjoyed sifting through boxes of Tanner's artwork all the way back to his elementary school years. Yep. I'm one of those moms. Each stick figure drawing made me smile as I re-lived the phases. I was committed to only taking those items that bring me joy, beauty, and ease. I wasn't going to hang on to anything out of a sense of obligation, guilt, or that I might "need this someday." I happily made many trips to Goodwill, sold furniture on Craigslist, and took even more to consignment. Now happily unpacking in my new place, in contrast to what others predicted about the horror and stress of it all, I can honestly say that the move was a fun adventure.

We get attached to our beliefs and easily confuse a long held belief with a fact. Would you categorize these as facts or beliefs?

> Mondays suck.
> The holiday season is busy and stressful.
> Teenagers are difficult.
> My body is falling apart as I age.
> Thank God it's Friday.
> Vacations are always too short.
> Relationships are difficult.

Being an empty nester is a tough transition.
There is never enough money.
The Millennials are lazy.
You can't have it all.
There is never enough time.

Stand guard at the entrance to your mind and pay attention to which beliefs and rules enter. Question what you tell yourself.

Allow yourself to defy the norm. Try walking into the office and saying, "Thank God it's Monday. This week is going to rock!" You should have seen the reactions I got when my response to people's comments about my move was, "Moving is so fun; I'm loving the adventure." People thought I was either in denial or losing my mind, but that wasn't the case. I was being completely honest.

Be willing to re-check the beliefs you've had about yourself for years (Afraid of heights? Don't like artichokes? Terrible at math?). If it is something you decided years ago, is that rule worth testing again to see whether it still holds true, or if you can let it go?

PRACTICE:

Here are some questions to use as you assess whether you want to keep the rule or throw it out:
- Is this a fact or a long held belief?
- Is this my belief or someone else's?
- If it is someone else, who gave it to me and when did I adopt is as mine?
- Does this rule now serve me or work against me?
- Are there examples of when this has not held true? (I bet you've had some wonderful Mondays!)

RULE #2
Life is Hard

RULE BREAKER
Let Go of the Struggle

Sometime in the 80s, the slogan "shit happens" became very popular and eventually was adopted as a life truth. On the one hand, we can all agree that yes, shit happens. Life doesn't go according to our plan much of the time. Unexpected events can throw us completely off track. On the other hand, let's take control of what we define as tough times. It seems we put a whole lot of things in the "shit" bucket that could be defined differently.

Some years ago, I realized that I used the word "struggle" frequently in every day conversations. It was a word I had picked up during my therapy days and a way to express empathy to others—as in, "I'm sorry that you are struggling with that." At some point it trickled into my daily vocabulary and out of habit, I over-used it for minor things that weren't really a struggle . Recently, when "back to school" season was in full swing, I also noticed how often I heard others use it in complaints like, "My son struggles with the transition from vacation to getting back on a school schedule," or "I'm struggling with summer being over."

When and how did the word "struggle" become so commonplace?

Yes, our challenges are real—in the prior example, some kids do have a tougher time with transitions, and I too feel sad when the summer season wraps up. There is no reason to deny reality. It's also important to acknowledge the emotions that come with transitions. But, really—a struggle? Maybe the word struggle is being used too freely. By definition, struggle means: "To contend with an adversary or opposing force"; "To advance with violent effort."

We can create different results by using different language. Over time, I eliminated using the word struggle, unless it was to describe a truly tough situation that wasn't easy to resolve and therefore causing me some emotional upheaval. Certainly, there are those life events that hit us on a deep emotional level and cause us pain, confusion and true struggle.

In my quest to be more conscious about what I called a struggle in my own life, I began by reminding myself of the continuum of struggles people experience across the world. There are women waking up in Africa this morning in need of water who will walk eight hours through unsafe territory, being vulnerable to assault and disease. If they find water, they'll carry forty-pound jerry cans on their back in hopes of returning to their families before dark. That's a struggle.

What of the story of Imaculee Ilibagiza, who spent ninety-one days hiding in a cramped bathroom during the Rwanda genocide, emerging to find almost her entire extended family had been brutally murdered? That's struggle. And yet, she went on to find a way to forgive the people who killed her loved ones.

Would we be comfortable or embarrassed if people in other parts of the world observed and listened to us for a day? Would we expect them to relate to and empathize with our struggles? We may be confusing struggle with privilege. If our biggest stressor is helping a second grader with his transition to third grade, that's not struggle, it is privilege. The privilege of having the time, energy and resources to spend on a relatively minor issue—one that every educated human being on the planet has experienced.

Being stressed with too much to do before a family vacation and struggling to get everything done? That's not struggle, it is privilege—having the time, energy, and resources to take a family vacation.

I invite you to become an observer of whether you regularly use the word struggle and determine if it's a good fit for you.

PRACTICE

If not, here are some tips for alternatives.

1. **Replace the word 'struggle' with something more positive.** I was at a workshop in which we were encouraged to use the phrase "I'm on the verge of a massive breakthrough..." Or, what about one of these: "I'm learning to manage..." "I'm getting better at..." "I'm finding new ways to..."

2. **Ask directly for what you need.** Have you gotten in the habit of saying you are struggling as a passive way to ask for help? Write down one thing that is challenging for you. What type of help do you need in order to overcome the obstacles and who could you ask for help? Be active in asking for what you need and want. Don't expect others to anticipate your needs.

3. **Play with possibilities.** Practice being more playful in your approach to problem-solving—generate possibilities that energize you, rather than deplete you. Ask yourself, if I weren't struggling with this, what would be different in my life? Then, look forward as you take action to reach the end result rather than staying in the muck of the current situation.

4. **Let it go.** Remember that your past does NOT equal your future. Is your reaction something from your past that

you are ready to let go of? Then, let it go! If you're not ready to let it go, what is the perceived payoff for continuing to tell yourself and others that you are stuck in the struggle? Sometimes there are unspoken benefits to being perceived as a victim.

5. **Find a role model.** Identify someone who appears to have mastered the very thing you are struggling with. Ask them for ideas about how they achieved their success. Then, take massive action on their recommendations! Later, drop them a note to thank them and follow up on how their suggestions had a positive impact on your life. Avoid continuing to talk about your issue if you are unwilling or un-ready to take action. Otherwise, you risk burning out your supports.

6. **Lend a Hand.** Find someone whose scenario looks tougher than your own. Take the time to ask them if they'd like help and carve out the time to do so. Solving problems in which you are not directly involved may jump start your creativity! Either way, you'll feel better while being useful and a part of someone's success.

7. **Revisit an experience from the past that you initially saw as a struggle but were able to transform into an opportunity.** Remember how that felt?

Try to be aware of when you are saying life is tough and that you are struggling. Practice choosing other words, other perspectives that would support your life being easier, and build your confidence in believing that you can handle the challenges that come your way. Notice how your words effect your thoughts and feelings.

RULE #3
It is Better to Give than to Receive

RULE BREAKER
Receiving is a Gift to Yourself and Others

Most of us learned from an early age that giving is important. Two-year-olds are taught to share their toys, teenagers are told not to be selfish, adults are praised for giving away time and money. There is a lot of focus on giving. Leaders, spiritual gurus, and philanthropists talk about it. Winston Churchill said, "It is more agreeable to have the power to give, than to receive." Giving is a huge value for me in my own life. I love the feeling I get from doing for others, being generous with people I care about and surprising them by giving in unexpected ways.

What about that power of receiving? Did anyone teach us about the art of receiving: the benefits of receiving, how to receive, ways to develop the habit of receiving? Receiving would be a valuable skill to teach, starting in preschool and continuing throughout our lives. Can you imagine what kinds of habits would be cultivated if we taught young children to say, "It feels good to be a receiver!" instead of just the rote "say your please and thank you's"? What if, in addition to being wonderful givers, we admired and complimented people on what gracious receivers they are?

How do you personally receive a compliment? Is it with ease and self-love? Or, is it accompanied with an urge to deflect and minimize the statement? How do you receive a gift? With a sense of knowing you deserve it and allowing yourself to savor it? Or, do you quickly turn your attention to how you might return it, re-gift it, and for whom it may be better suited? How do you receive money? Does it inspire a feeling of peace and abundance, knowing there is plenty more where that came from? Or, do you worry it won't be enough and start focusing on the lack? How do you receive love from yourself and others? Does it tend to come packaged in drama, conflict, and hardship? Or, are you showered with healthy love from yourself and others? Can you be fully authentic and stand up for yourself? Or, do you need to pretzel yourself into what others expect of you in order to receive the love that you want?

Although we may revere being great givers, the inability to receive comes at a cost, often contributing to fatigue, burnout, anger, resentment, and failed relationships. There was a meme going around Facebook recently that said, "You can't pour from an empty cup." We need to receive in order to replenish ourselves and have our needs met. It is healthy to be equally comfortable with receiving and giving. There are understandable reasons that most of us learned to shy away from receiving. In working with people over the years, I noticed that the reasons for being unaccustomed to receiving often fell into one of these categories:

- Someone mistreated or abused you early in life. You mistakenly interpreted that to mean something negative about you, resulting in believing that you were unworthy or undeserving. In reality, those events were actually a reflection of the other person and absolutely nothing about you.
- You grew up in a family where there was an unspoken rule that whomever had the least amount of needs would most easily survive. You became very skilled at having little or no needs and therefore, not being on the receiving end of much at all.

- Somewhere along the way, you got the message that what you did for others and what you accomplished were more important than who you are. You have since been very busy doing, achieving and setting goals ... leaving little room for being a receiver.

If receiving makes you uncomfortable, give some thought to what the payoff is for being a super giver. Do you play the martyr and feel good when people say that no one does as much, gives as much, works as much as you do? Do you benefit from holding the reputation for being the last one to leave the office? Are you on every committee and volunteer project? If so, at what cost? Don't fool yourself. There is always a cost! It might be your stress level, how much sleep you are able to give yourself, or it could be at the cost of your relationships not being authentic. If you consistently value giving more than you value being honest, there are times that you aren't really telling the whole truth.

As you move through the day, be an observer of yourself in situations where you have the opportunity to give and to receive. Take note of where you say yes and where you choose to say no. Notice whether it is a healthy balance of giving and receiving or if it feels more heavily weighted towards one or the other.

Any one of these moments can be a great time to practice saying yes even though you don't need it. You don't have to need the help or the gift being offered in order to say yes to receiving.

One of the skills of being a receiver is to take responsibility for asking for what you need and want. Not being able to do this in a direct and healthy way will leave you acting like a victim who wants others to read their minds. And, we know that's not going to go well.

My parents have been married for sixty-one years and every year since I can remember, when my mother's birthday rolls around in April, Dad asks her what she'd like for a gift or celebration. My Mom says, "Oh, you know I'm not much into birthdays. Let's be low-key about it." My Dad thinks she's telling the truth and follows her orders—low-key, nothing special. Inevitably, when I'm talking with my Mom in the days following her birthday, she complains that my Dad didn't do anything to make her birthday special. Doesn't he know that gift cards are so impersonal?

Finally, last year, I said to my Mom, "This seems ridiculous. Every year you are disappointed with Dad on your birthday. Why don't you tell him very directly what you'd like that would make for a good birthday?"

"Well, if I have to tell him, what's the point?" she said. Sound familiar? She felt it was my Dad's responsibility to know what would make her happy on her birthday and that telling him would make it less pleasurable.

We assume others are connecting the dots in our lives. If we've lived with them for this long or worked with them for ten years, don't they know what we need and want? Not necessarily. Most of us are too busy thinking about ourselves to become experts on what someone else desires.

Think about a current challenge you're having in your life—it could be a tough relationship, a work issue, a resentment. Like my mom, are you assuming the other person knows what you need and want? Any chance that a simple conversation to let them know directly could be a step in the direction of easing the tension?

Asking makes us vulnerable. Not asking makes us victims.

If you don't ask, then don't complain.

To Ask or Not to Ask...That is the Question

Other people may react strangely to us when we begin to ask for things. We never know what emotions or life experiences someone else is bringing to the table. We can't control other people's reactions but we can control our choice to speak up and ask.

The other day I stopped at a small chain grocery store to pick up a few items for lunch-on-the-go during a short break between meetings. When I got to the checkout with just three things, I realized there were no self-checkout or express lanes. Each lane was backed up at least six customers deep. After standing there for a few minutes, I walked up to one of the cashiers and with a smile, asked if there were additional cashiers to assist with the lines. Before the employee could answer, a customer who had just completed his checkout and was about to leave the store turned to me and angrily scowled, "Oh, stop it! You'll get over yourself." I was so stunned that I backed up and returned to my place in line.

The interaction stuck with me for a while as I thought, "How could that guy have been so upset by me asking for better service? Had he waited in line for a long time and felt that I should do the same? Did he think I was being difficult despite the fact that I was happy, respectful, and polite? Had he just gotten fired and was in a terrible mood?" I'll never know why he reacted so strongly to my request, but it did make me wonder—have we become so accustomed to lackluster service that we think it is inappropriate to ask for it to improve? Do we experience someone asking to have their needs met as a negative quality?

I wasn't highly attached to getting out of the grocery store more quickly, but I would have preferred to, and I was very comfortable asking. Similarly, when I'm renting a car or checking into a hotel, I almost always joke with the staff person while asking for a complimentary upgrade. Most often I get it, sometimes I don't. The outcome isn't as important to me as is the practice of asking for what I would like. I find it helpful to practice on the unimportant things so that when I do need to ask for something with higher stakes, I'm less hesitant to do so.

When we don't ask, and instead tell ourselves it doesn't matter, we are also saying that we don't matter—we don't deserve to have what we want. Waiting for other people to anticipate our needs is a perfect formula for feeling stressed, resentful, and angry. Emotions compound. What starts out as a minor event left unexpressed easily snowballs into a bigger deal by the many times we leave it unsaid. Finally, we blow a fuse. Then we are told that we are overreacting.

It is so much easier when we practice speaking up on the little things to build the muscle in preparation for asking for bigger things too.

PRACTICE

If you are interested in building the habit of receiving, consider starting with some small opportunities and practice saying yes, when:

- the grocery store bagger asks if you'd like help out to the car
- you are traveling and a fellow passenger asks if you'd like help getting luggage from the overhead bin
- a friend is making a trip to the store and asks if you need anything
- you're hosting a party and the guests ask if they can help
- you're swamped at work and a co-worker offers to take something off your plate

Any one of these moments can be a great time to practice saying yes even though you don't need it. Remember, you don't have to need the help or the gift being offered to you in order to say yes and receive it.

RULE #4
Don't Compare Yourself to Others

RULE BREAKER
Compare to Win

We've all heard "don't compare yourself to others," as if comparing is a bad thing. The way we use comparison is the real issue, not whether or not we do it. The truth is, whether we realize it or not, comparing ourselves to others is something we all do.

Much has been written suggesting that we should completely stop comparing ourselves. I disagree. It is in our human nature to want to know where we stand and how we rank. This desire probably goes back to the hunter and gatherer days when we had to know how we measured up to the hungry lion to survive. It may just go back to childhood, when we found ourselves being measured against a sibling or schoolmate. In any case, we can change the way and the "why" we compare so that it works to our benefit, helping us to grow rather than to devalue ourselves.

What are we really talking about when we talk about comparing ourselves to others? Start by thinking about whether you relate to these types of scenarios:

You are at a summer BBQ in conversation with someone you've just met. As you talk, topics of neighborhoods, schools, and jobs come up. Before you know it, you are no longer present in the conversation. Instead, your mind is calculating. This person lives in Cherry Hills and just took a vacation to Spain, therefore they must be in a higher income bracket than I am, and I bet they have a nicer home. She just mentioned that their kids go to a private school. I wonder what her husband does for work or if they have family money? I don't think I'll strike up a friendship with her because I'd be too embarrassed to have her see my house which isn't furnished as luxuriously as hers. I'll just walk away now and make excuses before our conversation goes any further.

You are at a business meeting and are enjoying talking to some new contacts in your industry. Quickly, you are mentally sizing up who makes more money, who is more successful, who went to the more prestigious school, who has climbed the corporate ladder more quickly. Instead of enjoying the camaraderie, you find your self-talk suddenly getting negative about why you're not performing at a higher level. As the interactions end, you leave the meeting feeling shame and discouragement because of the assumptions you're making about both your and their life.

You are a beginning writer and taking a class at the local arts center. Before the first week is over, you are already telling a story about the other people enrolled in the class. The woman in front with the Italian accent seems so confident. She probably already has an agent. The guy sitting next to you is twenty years younger than you, went to an Ivy League college and seems to have read the entire canon of English literature. You've never heard of half the writers he mentions on the first day. Before you've even gotten around to submitting your work or reading anybody else's, you are certain that every person in the room is a genius embarking on the great American novel and that you, with your trite little stories, are a fraud. You drop out after the second week.

These are a few everyday examples of how we use the habit of comparison to our detriment. Unfortunately, we tend to "compare to lose." When we do this, we are setting ourselves up to feel less than others and inadequate regardless of the situation. There are three key ways we do this:

1. **Weakness vs. Strength:** We take our weaknesses and compare them to someone else's strengths. For example, if I recently gained weight and I'm popping out of my clothes, I'm more likely to compare myself to a friend who is incredibly fit and loves doing triathlons, rather than comparing myself to someone who is dealing with obesity. We pose unrealistic expectations of ourselves to be at the finish line in something we've just begun.

2. **Internal vs. External:** We judge our internal reality and compare it to our perception of someone else's external reality. From a distance, without knowing the inner details, we idealize someone else's life and assume we have and are less. For example, our teenager is going through a tough phase, not doing well socially, and it's keeping us up worrying at night. We see on Facebook that a child of an acquaintance just won an award. Not knowing any of the details about that family, we secretly feel jealous of how things look so easy for them and wonder why we're not more like them. Social media has exacerbated this with a culture of "look at me at my best moments," without sharing the down and dirty truth behind those perfect scenes.

3. **Low vs. High:** We are most apt to compare when we are feeling emotionally low, rather than when we are on a high. The worst time to compare ourselves is when we're tired, dealing with a challenge, or experiencing a loss. It's a recipe for feeling worse and not seeing things accurately. When we're low, we see everything through a dark and distorted lens. Think about the last time you hit a high point in life. Maybe your family life was humming along and balanced

for a phase or maybe you just scored a big new client that was a huge professional win. When that happened, did you stop to congratulate yourself and acknowledge you accomplished something that many other people have not? If you didn't, you're not alone. Most of us choose to compare from a low, not from a high point.

I vividly remember a time in my life when I could have patted myself on the back for a courageous accomplishment but instead beat myself up mentally. I had just closed the doors on my private psychotherapy practice—motivated by a combination of feeling that after thirteen years in the business (and a significant degree of burnout), I had met my goals and needed to do something different.

As William Bridges says in his wonderful little book entitled *Transitions*, we don't generally go from an ending to a beginning. There is usually a "neutral zone" where we detach and hang out until we move to the next step. The neutral zone found me biking around the South Island of New Zealand where I spent a month exploring. Part of the trip was with a cycling group, and at the end of a long day, we had planned to end up at the bungee jumping in Queenstown. It was the first commercial bungee place in the industry and at that time, there wasn't a lot of fanfare with liability issues or instruction. We climbed to the historic Kawarau Bridge, paid our money, and they happily strapped our feet together with ropes and cables. While the jumper shuffled to the ledge of the bridge, the onlookers yelled, "Three – two – one!" in unison as the next person jumped 141 feet into the river below.

I was scared out of my mind. Not being a swimmer, nor considering myself athletic, and having a healthy fear of heights all added to the normal fear of jumping off a bridge. I was shaking.

I managed to flail myself off the bridge and found the top of my head brushing against the river water as I realized I was still alive. While some friends in the group thought it was pure fun and ran back up to do it again, I'd had all the adrenaline I could handle and was happy to check bungee jumping off my list of things to do. That night over dinner and drinks, we watched the videos of each of us jumping. Unlike my partners in crime, who were silly, playful, and graceful divers, my video clearly showed me about to pee in my pants and flapping through the air with absolutely no style. Rather than congratulating myself on the bravery of pushing past my fear, I felt embarrassed by my awkward performance and ridiculed myself in front of the group.

How many times do you do something that is pretty amazing but then in an instant, compare how you measured up to others? I call this "comparing to lose" because it sabotages our ability to feel good. It propels us down the emotional spiral of shame, embarrassment, discouragement or depression.

Every day, we have experiences where we are comparing ourselves to others without realizing the toll it takes on us. When we compare to lose, it takes away the option to feel good about who we are and what we've accomplished. We become too focused on the gap between where we are now and where we think we should be. Comparing to lose fuels feelings of low self-esteem and a sense of discouragement in that we can never measure up.

Logically, we understand that it is not helpful to compare ourselves to others in these negative ways. Emotionally, it is easy to get hooked. There are two types of triggers: those stemming from past pain (a familiar feeling from something in our past) or future pleasure (I want what you have). Once we become aware of our triggers, we can choose to use the information differently.

Past Pain	Future Pleasure
(A familiar feeling)	*(I want what you have)*
being compared to a sibling	material possessions
feeling left out	house
being abandoned / replaced by	car
someone else	travel
neglect and / or abuse	romantic relationships
loss and grief	lifestyle
experiencing rejection	sense of ease
being told you couldn't have or	family life
do something that	having / not having children
others could	business success
being told you weren't good	income
at something (especially	retirement
in comparison to some-	social circle
one else)	fitness level
feeling that you didn't	
measure up	
feeling alone	
shame / embarrassment	
not being listened to	

Let's take a look at those two categories. Triggers related to past pain might be something you've experienced in the past that led to comparison and it is now getting triggered again. Example: you were compared to your sister when you were growing up and now you're being compared to a co-worker. The intensity of the feeling is stronger because it is stirring up the past. A common feeling for me in my childhood was that I didn't fit in. As an adult, when I'm in a social or business setting that triggers the feeling of "I don't fit in here", it can become much more intense than is warranted for the current situation because of what it is reminding me of from the past.

Triggers that are about future pleasure revolve around you wanting something that someone else has. It's common these days to 'joke' about having envy — "I'm having house envy, vacation envy, car envy, etc". Seeing someone have something we would like to have can trigger a negative emotion — I want that! How come she has it and I don't? The problem isn't in wanting what someone else has, it is in thinking that we can't have it.

In a step towards changing your tendency to negatively compare yourself with others, take an observer role and act as a detective collecting clues. When do you feel triggered to compare? What types of people are more likely to trigger you to feeling inadequate? These are clues to what you are craving more of in your life. That couple from church that seems to always be returning from an exotic vacation? Could it be that you are craving having more adventure and travel with your spouse? Rather than focusing on the other person, make a note to yourself about what you are discovering. If it is more adventure that has triggered your jealousy, you could start with small steps rather than thinking you need to take an international vacation. Trying a new restaurant or a night away locally may be a good first step.

You might say to yourself, "Here I go, I'm feeling jealous about this again. Why is this getting me stirred up?" Rather than focusing on the other person, we can begin to practice self-awareness and self-love. Instead of comparing to lose, we can choose to turn it into a game by asking, "How can I use this information to move myself up the ladder of positive feelings?" rather than going down the dreaded spiral of emotional shame and despair.

As we notice our envy and self-deprecating thoughts, all of which feel crappy, we can shift to "comparing to win" by experimenting with new thought patterns.

Build your belief in abundance rather than scarcity. Often we are in the mindset of wanting something that another person

47

seems to have. That's fine because there is plenty for all of us. They can have it and so can I. We are not in competition. There is not a limit on how many people get to be fit in this lifetime or how many people are able to enjoy a healthy relationship. As you notice what someone else has, remind yourself that the very fact that they have it, means that you can have it too.

Value your own uniqueness and don't compare and crave something that you don't actually have a high value for. My friend Leesa is an amazing cook, quilter, and skilled at so many different—one of those people who can knit a little something, put it in the washing machine and it comes out as a beautiful felted purse that looks straight off the shelf from a hip boutique. I know how to do absolutely none of those things. I'm not interested in them and I imagine I would not have any natural skill. I did grow up in a family who enjoys traveling internationally and I'm very comfortable with planning an adventure and leaving the country. Leesa often wishes she traveled more, yet she doesn't enjoy it. Despite her repeated experience of having a bad time on vacation, she continues to plan trips for herself and her husband. Inevitably, she returns home with a disaster story—they went to take a cruise leaving from Miami and it got cancelled due to a a hurricane. They went to Maui and it rained the entire time. They went to Ireland and got sick from the food (who gets sick on potatoes, beer, and beef?). Leesa is placing a high value on travel because she has seen others enjoy it. Yet, she may be happier if she were able to admit that she finds more joy being home doing her crafts and let go of the belief that her life would be more fulfilling if she learned to travel well. When you find yourself comparing, ask yourself: Is this something you really value or is it a comparison that doesn't serve you? The more authentic we are, the less it matters what others are doing and having.

Let's not blame ourselves or feel guilty about comparing. Instead, let's be observers and use the information we gain as a guide to steer us towards our best lives.

PRACTICE

I feel jealousy / envy when I'm around people who

The specific triggers that I most relate to are:

Taking this new observer role, I am now aware that those triggers may be clues that I am craving more:

Some simple action steps I can take towards my needs and wants (as identified in the previous question)

RULE #5
Don't Show Off

RULE BREAKER
It's OK to Shine...In Fact, That's What You're Here to Do!

When you were growing up, did you repeatedly hear certain rules from the adults in your life? One common rule in my era was that we shouldn't need or want attention on ourselves. "Don't show off!"

Adults were worried that too much attention on a child would make them spoiled and self-centered. Parents themselves had been raised with the theory that children should be seen but not heard. Not "showing off" was one way to avoid grooming those negative qualities. There is a big difference between showing off and feeling good about who we are. We may have interpreted those childhood messages to mean that we should stay out of the limelight and hence, minimize who we are. How does this play out in your life now as an adult? Do you dress to make sure you don't draw attention to yourself? Do you downplay your accomplishments because you don't want other people to think you are "full of yourself"? Do you hold yourself back in what you say and do in hopes of not offending others? Take note of whether you are using these as ways to dim your personal power.

The tall poppy syndrome is a social phenomenon where people criticize and resent those whose accomplishments elevate them above their peers. Instead of trying to rise to a higher level and joining them, some people try to drag the elevated person (the tall poppy) down to their lower level. You may have heard of this same principle in the classic analogy of the pot of crabs. A bucket full of live crabs doesn't need a cover on it because the crabs won't get out. If one or more crabs try to escape by crawling up and out, their crab buddies will be sure to pull them back down into the bucket to remain trapped together.

Most cultures have their own version of this philosophy. The Scandinavians have the Law of Jante which discourages individual success and places a higher value on the collective. The theme of the Law of Jante is that you should not believe you are special and there are ten rules to follow that all support this idea. The Japanese have a saying: "The nail that sticks out gets hammered down".

Another version is the classic "Misery loves company." If you have been single and have commiserated with your single friends about how horrible the dating process is, don't be surprised if when you fall in love, those same friends try to ruin your new buzz. They may want to keep you in a stuck place with them rather than celebrate your newfound happiness.

Most families have a thermostat on their norm for happiness levels, income levels, quality of relationships, and lifestyle. Unknowingly, we may try to play small so that we don't stand out as having surpassed our parents or our siblings. It's not uncommon to feel guilty or self-conscious if you attain a higher level of success, income or happiness than the rest of your family has experienced. You can choose to bring this out in the open. Have honest conversations with the people close to you about the choices you are making to improve your own life, and how that doesn't change the value you place on your relationship with them. Ultimately, you may need to choose between your highest good and the approval of others.

Being Responsible as an Excuse to not Rise to your Full Potential

Most adults would agree that being responsible is a good thing. Being responsible is doing what is expected of us and being a reliable and predictable person. Oftentimes that's true. Sometimes, though, responsibility is a tempting excuse for choosing to play it safe and not rise to our full potential. It's easy to play the responsibility card as the reason we're not doing whatever would be more authentic, more life affirming. In doing so, we choose the victim role: "Poor me, I'm just so responsible or I would make some changes." Are you using this as a creative way to not step into your best life? It's a safe option, because no one is likely to argue with you about being responsible. On the contrary, you may get praise and accolades for how much you sacrifice.

Some of the typical ways we play the responsibility card rather than choosing to break the rules are seen in the following scenarios:

Knowing that your relationship has been troubled for a long time but saying you can't leave because of your joint retirement funds, the kids, or your health insurance. You convince yourself that it wouldn't be responsible to break up the family. You don't want to cause anyone pain. This allows you to stay safe and avoid having tough conversations, potential conflicts, and massive change.

You're in a safe job that pays adequately and is secure. You hate it, and are counting the years to retirement. Rather than start a job search and create new possibilities, you talk about how it wouldn't be responsible to leave a "good" job and give up your position. This allows you to avoid the stress and risk involved in a job hunt as well as avoiding the possibility of feeling rejected or like a failure in the event you aren't hired by another company.

You have an aging parent who needs care and none of your siblings are stepping up to help. You take on more of the role of caretaker than you want and vent about how responsible you are and how wrong your siblings are to put all the burden on you. This allows you to play the victim role and not take personal responsibility for setting healthy limits on what you are willing to do.

Your kids are old enough to make their own lunch, do their laundry, and a lot more around the house. You continue to over- function so that they can under-function and hide it under the umbrella of how it is just part of being a responsible parent. This doesn't allow you to free up that time to explore what you need and want, make a career change, take time to exercise and get in shape, or whatever else you are wanting but avoiding.

Begin to notice situations and roles in which you've assumed you're being responsible. Is that the full truth, or are you also hiding from something because it scares you and it is more comfortable to stay stuck than to break the rules of not drawing attention to yourself?

PRACTICE:

Reflect on how you were encouraged to either show up fully or conversely, to not draw attention to yourself. What messages did you internalize and from whom? Where did you learn to stop yourself?

Have conversations with trusted family members about the topic of the family thermostat as it relates to happiness, fitness, income – or whatever categories are relevant to you. What is the family norm? What feelings are there about exceeding those norms? Could there be agreement to support each other in releasing those limits?

Look for opportunities to stand out a bit more than you might have in the past:
- Do you look in your closet and see a sea of sensible black and grey clothes but you secretly love bright orange and reds? Buy yourself something that is more true to your preferences. Wear something that feels more bold than usual. Notice how you feel and what sort of comments you may get from others.

- Do you hesitate to speak up in meetings? Try voicing an opinion even if your voice cracks and you turn red in the face. You may fight the urge to write it off as not important enough to speak up. Do it anyways. It will get easier with practice over time.

- Do you nod in agreement rather than openly disagree because you don't want to cause a conflict or offend someone? This could be another opportunity to not tone down your true self and instead, take the risk to be authentic and state your opinions.

- You are the only one in history who can deliver your exact gifts, your voice, your unique perspective—all of which are needed in the world. You are here to shine fully, not to hide, shrink or show up as a watered-down version of your beautiful self.

RULE #6
Keep a Busy Schedule

RULE BREAKER
*Slow Down and Enjoy
Your Own Company*

With the hectic pace we keep these days, it takes a special effort to find time for ourselves. If we are unaccustomed to time alone, it can feel daunting.

When I was early in my single parenting days, Tanner went to summer camp for a month. In the first few days after he left, I felt dazed. With no one who needed my immediate attention and a lot more flexible time, I found myself walking around the house wondering what exactly I should be doing. As time progressed, I learned to look forward to my solo time as a great opportunity to rejuvenate and create some open space to think, and sometimes that meant doing a lot of nothing—not judging my day based on my productivity level.

Do you book yourself solid with activities from morning to night without a break? Do you often feel you don't have enough time or that days are flying by and you're not sure what you are "getting done?" At some point in the last couple of decades it became very trendy to be busy. Instead of spontaneously getting together with friends, it became commonplace to say, "I'd love to get together but we're so busy. What about next month?" It has become more rare for people to pop in on each other for a spontaneous coffee and instead to spend enormous amounts of time trying to coordinate one social date while everyone tries to sync their hectic calendar. For some people, being busy has become a status symbol and a way to fit in.

In addition to our own busy calendar, scheduling our kids and/or families came next. I grew up in a small town neighborhood that boasted over fifty kids in a one square block radius (ok, admittedly, my family was nine of those). Every night during the warm months, all we needed to do was go out the backdoor to find plenty of kids to form a baseball team or play other outdoor games. These days, with kids in ninety-nine activities every week, most parents and children don't have down time. It's no wonder that as adults, we have not had the opportunity to become at ease in the stillness and the quiet. Unless you have made it a conscious choice or have a meditation practice, you may not ever experience sitting in quiet. When you do have a few minutes of free time, it's likely you feel that you should be getting something done. Doing nothing is not valued. If you want time to do nothing and become familiar with spending time with yourself void of activity, you'll need to claim that right and make the time.

As with any of these new habits, enjoying your own company may feel strange and pointless. With practice, you'll begin to reap the benefits of cultivating the best version of yourself. It's tough to be at our best when we are constantly "on".

When Tanner was in kindergarten, I went on a class camping trip as one of the chaperone parents helping the teachers. Twenty-two five-year-olds in tents. Pouring rain. All night long. Tired kids, wet clothes, no fire for hot chocolate or s'mores. By the time we got home and I unpacked the gear, I felt completely wiped. I said to my husband, "I'm going to a nice hotel. I'm not sure which one but I'll call you."

I checked myself into the Loews Giorgio, which at that time was a huge splurge for our budget. Because it was so last minute, the only room they still had available was one of the suites. As the bell captain and I were in the elevator on the way up, he said, "What brings you to Denver?"

"I live here."

There was a long silence. Then, as he showed me around the suite, he said, "Should you have company tonight, the door to the living room does close for privacy." After he left, I flopped on the bed laughing. Clearly, he had seen my wedding ring and thought I was plotting a secret rendezvous. I put on my white robe, had room service deliver risotto and a glass of wine and sat on my king size bed with crispy clean sheets. In less than an hour, I felt so much happier, I almost wanted to go home and see my boys.

I called Garry to tell him where I was (and why!), to which he was totally supportive and said, "Enjoy, I got you covered. See you tomorrow." Sometimes we have to be selfish in order to be sustainable. I could have been a victim and gone home and done laundry and other things, feeling totally depleted. It was one of the best decisions I ever made and looking back on it, I have drawn energy from remembering how good it felt, and that it was a bold statement about taking care of myself.

We don't always need a big vacation or a luxury suite. It might be asking your partner to get out of the house (and take the kids with them!) while you have an afternoon to yourself to enjoy the quiet. Or, it could be that on the way home from work you take an hour detour at the library and enjoy reading free magazines in a big comfy chair. Don't expect other people to encourage you to take care of yourself. You train others how to treat you. If you're not willing to take excellent care of yourself, no one else will do it for you. If you have children, keep in mind you are modeling for them how to take care of themselves.

The surprising outcome of doing less and taking time to relax is that it fuels us in a way that allows us to be more productive in the long run. We feel less tired and less resentful. There is a saying: "What you resist, persists." In other words, if you resist slowing down, all the drawbacks will persist. If you are determined to continue going at a breakneck pace, sacrificing sleep and quiet at the expense of your happiness, then it will be terribly challenging to create a life you love. We are humans, not robots. We are not meant to be in motion every minute of the day.

You may not like the idea of being alone with no one to talk with. You may not feel you need quiet. I encourage you to try it and learn it as a skill. It can result in creative thoughts and ideas, more energy, and discovering what you need and want. Try it as an experiment—even if for twenty minutes—and note how you feel.

Zip It!

Do you wake up to a jolting alarm, turn on the TV, radio, or music? The kids are making noise. There's traffic noise. My neighbor's dog is barking as I write this. Noise is pervasive these days. Every restaurant and store we go into has their own music blaring. I often wonder what it would be like to have an annual "Zero Noise Pollution Day" where all retailers, businesses, and individuals agree to twenty-four hours of quieting the background noise. We're plugged in to our own devices for constant noise. The only time we really experience stillness is when we camp, hike, or somehow get into nature, but how often is that?

It takes courage to go against the norm and decrease the chatter and noise level around us. When we do, amazing things can grow out of that calm. Before we learn to speak up, we need and benefit from learning to be quiet. Many of us are afraid of having quiet time and avoid it at all costs. How often when someone is quiet, we ask them, "Is something wrong?"

In lobbies and waiting rooms we all stare at our devices, often with our headphones on, rather than tolerating the unfamiliar quiet. In elevators, we face the door and pretend we're not uncomfortable in the silence and being in close quarters with strangers. Whether it be Starbucks, the grocery store, or the gas station, there is music in the background. In our cars, we have the music blaring or talk on our phones rather than savoring the cocoon we're in and the potential quiet. Have you ever been at one of those gas stations that while you're filling up your tank, a video surprisingly comes on shouting at you to buy some sort of additive? It scared the crap out of me the first time and I jumped—until I found the mute button. What in the world...is there no place that is immune to the constant chatter?

Have you heard of the five-hour energy drinks, the little bottles you see at checkout counters? The man who invented those, Manoj Bhargava, made billions of dollars from the invention, and is now using his wealth to create solutions to the planet's most pressing issues including water, energy, and health. I was interested to learn that he was a monk for twelve years. Although I haven't met him, I imagine it's not a coincidence that he spent many years being quiet before he entered a decade of doing incredibly innovative and amazing feats. Could he have done that amid noise and chaos, not being able to think? I doubt it.

The Art of Listening

Listening is such a gift. In my corporate programs, I often include a simple exercise. Two people sitting together turn to each other. One talks for three minutes. The other person can't interrupt, ask questions, take notes, or comment. When the three minutes are up, they reverse so that the other one gets a turn to talk. Repeatedly, attendees say they have never experienced that—never experienced being listened to for 180 seconds. Crazy!

Is there someone in your life right now who is posing challenges for you? I dare you to sit with them and do nothing but listen for a few minutes. It could change your life. I'm not kidding.

> "Most people do not listen with the intent to understand; they listen with the intent to reply."
>
> *Stephen R. Covey*

Usually, especially in the workplace, listening is paired with problem-solving as natural companions. Going directly from listening to problem-solving skips over the most critical step of the process, which is being curious. Listen in order to create curiosity. Embrace an attitude of "What if?" From a place of curiosity and openness comes a natural flow of solutions and action.

Listening to ourselves is equally important. If you never give yourself the opportunity to be with your thoughts or listen to what comes up, how can you even know what you truly want and need? We have been trained our whole lives to believe that other people have the answers. When we get quiet, we realize that we do in fact have a lot of inner knowing and wisdom.

As you try spending a bit of time alone and having some quiet, you may become more aware of how you talk to yourself in private. Research suggests that we have about 60,000 thoughts a day. The vast majority of those are not conscious. Imagine if you could record your thoughts throughout the day. What are you saying to yourself? Are you a loving, encouraging coach or a mean and critical boss to yourself?

Begin to pay attention to your self-talk and consciously choose words and conversations that support you.

Creating Quiet

Eat your meals without background noise. Turn off the TV, the radio, and have everyone turn off their phones. I was raised in a big family, the third oldest of nine kids. My Dad, a very gentle and mellow guy, was uncharacteristically strict about our dinner hour. He didn't allow calls from friends (back then, it was the landline plugged into the wall), and if anyone rang the doorbell while we were at the dinner table, he answered and told them that we were in the middle of a family dinner and wouldn't be available for one hour. Going around the table, each of us had to talk briefly about one thing we learned that day. If we couldn't identify something or were being rebellious by not wanting to talk, Dad would calmly ask us to go to the study where he had a set of Encyclopedia Britannica (for young readers: these were huge informational books, pre-google) and find something of interest to talk about. It was important to my parents that we had time around the table to talk and to listen without outside distractions.

When you are in the car, turn off the radio and your phone. You're in a little space where you have a lot of control over the amount of noise coming at you. There will be plenty of noise and distraction from traffic, sirens, other people, and honking, but take control of creating a quiet environment within your own car. If you habitually have the music cranking, give yourself the experience of how you feel without it.

Have a quiet morning. Do you turn on the TV to hear the news first thing in the morning? See how you feel without it for one week and then re-evaluate. Do you feel more peaceful or do you miss the noise? Remember the earlier story of the wasp trap? It is highly likely that the first few times you try to be in the quiet, it will feel as though you are headed in the wrong direction and that you are wasting time. Continue to experiment before jumping back to your old ways.

Mindfulness. This has become a mainstream topic. More companies are incorporating meditation and other mindfulness practices in the workplace. Research consistently shows that there are lots of benefits, including improving one's ability to deal with stress. If the idea of meditating isn't appealing or may be intimidating, try setting your stopwatch for one minute of quiet. Let that be a beginning to experience mindfulness. There are also a lot of great free apps that offer guided meditations with a variety of themes.

PRACTICE

When I consider having less noise in my life, it seems it would

_____

_____

_____

One thing that I am willing to do now to experiment with having more quiet time in my life is :

_____

_____

_____

If I change my habits to take time to unplug, the people who may not support me in doing that would be:

_____

_____

_____

Rule #7
Be Informed

RULE BREAKER
Don't Intake What You Won't Impact

What do you choose to fill your brain with? Do you turn on the TV to catch the gory accidents of the day, the random shootings, and updates on who left their child in a hot car? Let me ask you—how is that contributing to your life?

People's typical response to this question is, "It's good to be informed." Really? It's good to be informed of every horrible act occurring? How so? Does it help you to be more kind? Happier? Hopeful? Reach your goals?

Take any one thing—news, sports, reality TV shows. Let's say you regularly watch TV for 30 minutes a day. That amounts to three and a half hours a week or 182 hours a year. What if you had instead, used that time to read, garden, meditate, listen to a loved one, or pursue a business idea? Turning the TV off requires the courage to break the rules. Your partner, family, and friends may think it odd that you want space to do one of these activities rather than continuing the habit of dozing in front of the TV in the evening with them. Stepping back may trigger others to try and court you back into your old habits so that they have your company while they continue the norm of zoning in front of useless shows.

Everyone complains about not having enough time, but if you tally the use of time for gossip, reality TV, watching other people play sports, and surfing social media, it adds up to the difference between a mediocre and an amazing life. It has been calculated that the average American, if they live to be 73 years old, will have watched the equivalent of more than nine years of TV. Wow—nine years of your life—gone! If you love sports or are a news junkie and it brings you lots of joy, that's great. I'm not suggesting we should eliminate things that bring us joy. But, be conscious about where you focus your attention. If you are doing what everyone else is doing simply because everyone else is doing it, not because you love it, you are focusing on the wrong thing. Start paying attention to how you feel emotionally and physically after watching a game, the news, or binging on Netflix. Do you feel inspired and motivated? Tired and lazy? Depressed?

We recently survived a tense election season in the United States. Regardless of whether your candidate won or lost, I think most of us will remember it as an unusual one. It is generally agreed that it's good to vote and exercise the privilege given to us. There was a time in my life when I would have whole-heartedly agreed with that. These days, I edit that belief. It is important to vote if you are well informed—beyond reading newspaper headlines and watching biased TV shows that support your ideas. Have you researched the candidates? Do you have a deep knowledge of both sides of the issue? Are you voting with the party your family has voted for since the beginning of time because that's "what we've always done?" When someone with opposing views is expressing themselves, do you defend why you're right and they are wrong? Do you see the other parties as evil? If so, consider not voting so blindly. Take the time to understand the issues and educate yourself.

Why vote from a place of ignorance? Most Americans cannot accurately describe how our government works, our history, or our relationships with other countries, and yet we argue intensely about the issues. Maybe your time is better spent reading about the three branches of our government, understanding the Constitution and its Amendments, or what qualities have made for good leaders throughout history. Sit down for a coffee with people who have very different views from yours. Listen more than you talk. Take some notes.

I have a personal motto that I only intake what I can impact. Call me selfish, but if I am not going to donate money, volunteer to help, or do something with the information I've gained, then I don't allow it to take up space in my brain. I'd rather fill my mind with something positive and uplifting, and something that I can influence. What about you?

If you're brave, ask someone who loves you about how they experience you—do they regularly experience you as uplifting, energized and hopeful, or are you a ball of negativity?

Have you ever stopped to consider that the media is a business? In the early days, the media was to report the news in a fair manner. These days, it is much more competitive and skewed. Newspapers and magazines, TV and radio stations, make their profits by getting consumers to read, watch and buy their content. The way that they do this is very strategic. They capture the attention of their audiences (you and me) by creating anxiety and then giving a teaser that if you hang in there, they'll resolve the drama for you. Do you know what's poisoning you in your food? Stay tuned and we'll tell you the #1 thing you need to know to avoid getting cancer. The more people that stay tuned to watch, the better the ratings and profits. The media calls it: "If it bleeds, it leads". They are continually looking for headlines that play into our worry and fear. Creating more anxiety, we stay tuned for the resolution, and get a few moments of relief before the next news sensation follows. A baby drowns in a swimming pool in New Zealand. Stay tuned to hear what could have prevented it. We can all agree that a baby drowning is sad and heart breaking. But, what does it do for us to know that, other than to continue our cycle of fear and worry? Oh, and also to have a horrible story to keep re-telling at the office all day. Did you hear about Baby Mindy who drown in the swimming pool in Queenstown? Wasn't that sad? We were not built to carry the emotional burden of awareness about every single thing going on in the world about which we can do absolutely nothing. Take back control of your focus and therefore, your emotions. Why are you allowing the media to decide what you know, how you feel, what information you digest? Trust me, you are worth more than that and deserve to make your own choices.

Personally, I have not owned a television for over ten years. I know this is considered very extreme by most people and it continues to shock those who visit my home. But, for me it has freed up enormous amounts of time and energy for things that I value more than T.V. I love waking up to the quiet moments of the early morning, listening to positive podcasts, meditating, or watching uplifting videos and inspirational stories on my computer. Again, it is about making very individual and personal choices that fit our own internal compass, rather than doing what is expected of us. Only you can decide what fuels you in a positive direction.

Mind Your Own Business

At the beginning of the book, we talked about how some things have become so habitual, we don't even recognize them as a habit. Certain things can feel like "that's the way life is," and everybody does it. Change requires that we recognize when a habit doesn't serve us, and make the decision to replace it with something healthier. One of these habits is how we talk about other people.

Focusing on others, assuming we know how they should behave, and being in judgment about their choices, is a habit that has become too familiar and comfortable. Start examining whether you feel good about the way you talk about others and whether it is helping you to move towards or further away from living a life of ease and integrity. Here are some practical and do-able tips:

Adopt the philosophy that you don't talk about anyone unless they are present in the room to hear it. The exception is to give compliments—be generous in your praise of others regardless of whether they are there. Imagine the conflict that could be eliminated if we never spoke about someone without them being there to participate—i.e., no backstabbing, gossip, or communication blunders.

Stop yourself if you are about to talk negatively about someone. Go within yourself and check in with what is happening with you and why you want to spread ill will. Is there a way you could go to the person directly if there is something to be worked out?

Are you repeating stories about other people's drama or trauma? What purpose does that serve? If they were standing there with you, would they be pleased with the information you're reporting? Social media has certainly exacerbated all of this. A friend recently came to me and asked my permission to post a particular photo of me taken while I was working. I thought that was such a dignified and elegant thing to do. Don't assume others want their personal life broadcasted.

We have become a society that enjoys focusing on reality TV, watching the lives of others and feeling as though we know them personally. When you are standing in the line at the grocery store and tempted to pick up the most recent *People* magazine (who can resist those tempting teaser headlines?), take a step away from the magazine rack and ask yourself: How am I choosing to star in my own life? If there were a headline about my life (or my day, my week) what might it be?

Focusing on others instead of ourselves relates to the courage to be alone—whether that is alone in our thoughts, alone in our company, alone in our focus. Every time our focus is on judging or criticizing someone else, it is a lost opportunity to use that time to improve your own life. Focusing on other people—unless we are helping them or celebrating them—doesn't lead to our own personal happiness. Personally, I've found that when I'm being most critical of others correlates with the times I'm not feeling good about myself. When we're happy and living the life we want, there isn't much reason to criticize other people.

WHAT ABOUT YOU?

Are you playing by the rules and taking in what you can't impact? Consider the following and then decide if this is an area you want to change or if you feel good about where you're at:

- You have a routine that includes crashing in front of the TV at a certain time of day (first thing when you get home from work or right after dinner) and it doesn't feel fun. You feel increasingly tired and unmotivated rather than energized, entertained, or inspired by what you are taking in.
- You are able to recite a variety of negative incidents each morning that you saw on the news or read in the paper. None of the information has anything to do with you nor anything to do with action you plan to take.
- You repeat a lot of criticisms of politicians, celebrities, special interest groups, your employer, your church, etc. but you've been complaining about the same things for years and it hasn't changed your behavior.

- You find yourself gossiping a lot and talking behind other people's backs. You are minding other people's business more than you are minding your own.

PRACTICE:

Do a personal assessment of your relationship with TV, news and social media. Does it feel like a positive factor in your life or are there any changes you'd like to make? It could be a simple as cutting out one show to do something more fulfilling or to cut back on social media and see how you feel.

Practice giving compliments freely as well as choosing silence over criticism.

Ask yourself these questions before you tell a story you've repeated more than once:
- Is the story true?
- Is it uplifting?
- Is it relevant to the listener?
- Is it helping to shine a positive light on the people in the story?
- Would whomever it is about be happy that you are repeating it?
- Are you breaking any confidences in sharing it?

RULE #8
Act Your Age

RULE BREAKER
Don't Use Age as an Excuse

When asked in the past, I would tell people my age and then pause, waiting for the "Wow, you don't look forty," or fifty, or whatever age I was at the time. I liked those comments—they gave me the feeling that I'd beat the clock a bit and was somehow ahead of the game.

As I get older, I rarely get those comments. It initially disappointed me. I thought I had lost my lead! Crazy thinking, right? These days, when someone does say, "Oh, you don't look fifty-eight," my new response is, "This is what fifty-eight looks like."

The women's magazine called MORE, used to have a monthly column entitled, "This is what 60 (or 70, or 80) Looks Like," featuring a photo and short bio of a woman who not only looked great physically but was also shattering age myths in her hobbies or professional life. I loved reading that page to keep expanding my own view of the limitations I was falsely accepting as I age.

We have a visual image of each age—an image based on what that used to mean. At eighty-five years, my sweet grandmother was overweight, her breasts drooping down to her belly in her flowered housedress as she shuffled around in thick flat shoes. She had been a farmer and raised ten children with almost no money. Later, in her smaller house, she had an incredible garden and she was amazing at canning fruits and vegetables every year. Yet, she didn't have the benefits of much of what we know now about diet, cardio exercise, sunscreen, and so on. What eighty-five looked like for my grandma was based on the knowledge and habits of those times. Many of us are the first generation who have had the luxury of being physically active our whole life, whether through organized sports, walking, doing Zumba, or lifting weights. We're the first generation who had access to information about best nutritional habits, effects of over-consuming sugar or alcohol, and the benefits of cardio exercise. We're the first generation who has felt that therapy, counseling, and self-care are within reach. Wouldn't it stand to reason that we may age differently in body, mind, and spirit than our parents and grandparents did?

Along with some of the privileges we've had, there are also responsibilities (haven't we always told our kids that?). We can choose to take responsibility for the excuses we make as we age. I'm guilty of using my age as an excuse for not mastering technology, and I'm very slow to adopt new gadgets. But what about Olive Riley, who started her blog at age 107? Not being computer literate nor being able to see well enough to type, she had help from a gentleman who later made a documentary about her life. There are still videos of Olive on YouTube. This is what 107 looks like.

Have you started to say that you can no longer participate in certain sports and that your body is "falling apart" as you age? What about Tao Porchon-Lynch, who at ninety-nine years old, teaches eight yoga classes a week and says, "I don't put fear or decay in my mind." Or, the seventy-year-old Australian grandfather, Cyril Baldock, who swam the English Channel and then celebrated with a couple of beers "for medicinal purposes." This is what seventy looks like.

Do you have a business dream that you haven't acted on and now think it is too late? You can't afford to take the risk, you're too old, you're too settled in your career? What about Marc Guberti, who didn't care about age and as a high school student started an online business. He now publishes a book a month and has over 275,000 followers on Twitter. As he says, "You don't have to be eighteen or over to be successful." This is what eighteen years old looks like.

For everything you're saying you can't do, there's someone else out there who is overcoming their inner obstacles and doing it. Let's chip away at the chunks of excuses holding us back. This is what a rewarding life looks like.

PRACTICE

Is there something you think you are too young or too old to do?

_____

_____

_____

_____

If you were to argue the other side of the coin, why may that not be true? Is there someone else who has done it regardless of age?

_____

_____

_____

_____

What is one action you could take this week to move in the direction of busting through your limiting beliefs about age on this issue?

RULE #9
Don't Air Your Dirty Laundry

RULE BREAKER
Go Naked

In my years as a psychotherapist, I spent days listening to people's most private secrets behind closed doors. The events, habits, behaviors, personality traits, losses, addictions, or family trauma that made them feel at least flawed, if not unlovable and unworthy.

Instead of only talking behind closed doors, we can choose to expose ourselves to those we trust. We'd then realize that everyone has some degree of those feelings of shame and embarrassment—of not being enough. Welcome to the human species! We are not machines. We are amazing and wonderful, evolved beings who are capable of making plenty of mistakes, creating drama and trauma, and making less than stellar choices. The propensity to do all of these is exactly what makes us human, loveable and worthy.

One of my favorite stories as a kid was *The Emperor's New Clothes.* You might remember it—the emperor hires two weavers to create a luxurious outfit for him. No one in the village wants to admit they can't see the new clothes because that deems them as stupid. So, they all ooh and aah over how amazing the clothes are. Everyone is going along with the pretenses until a kid blurts out that the emperor is naked! Similarly, we may try to convince others that our lives are perfect by donning luxurious externals rather than getting naked with reality.

People who look the most put together are often the ones experiencing a lot of emotional pain. There may be reasons they put so much energy into making things look picture perfect. I'm usually a bit suspicious of the "perfect" family or couple. How many times have you heard of a divorce and people's response is: "Oh, they seemed like such a perfect couple!" In another scenario, someone commits suicide and we hear: "They had so much going for them, so much to live for." From an outside perspective, it may have looked good, but it certainly wasn't how it felt to that person from inside their own turmoil. Most families have some form of mental illness, addictions, abuse, affairs, trauma, or secrets hidden somewhere in their family tree. All that tells us is that they're human. Nothing more and nothing less.

Transparency doesn't mean that we go around telling our life story on a first meeting with someone or oversharing our innermost thoughts prematurely. It doesn't negate the value of therapy and talking privately about some issues. It is also not about being a victim and crying "poor me." Instead, transparency is a decision to allow our human-ness to show through rather than hiding it.

It may feel safe to have a false sense of predictability and certainty. People may know you as the super capable person that you are and you understandably like them having that image. You don't want to taint it with letting them know you have flaws and have made mistakes. Yet, it takes energy to keep up the façade and not allow yourself to be fully authentic.

You have experienced this. The voice in your head has you thinking that there is that thing (yes, that thing!) that makes you undesirable. Getting naked with it and not hiding it is likely to expose your real-ness, your relatability, and your vulnerability. If you knew that every single person has what could be considered a "flaw" and that no one escapes the human experience, would it encourage you to put your mask down and reveal your true self?

As you take the steps to reveal more of who you really are, you may find that you can connect with people in a more meaningful and healthy way.

> Today you are You, that is truer than true. There is no
> one alive who is Youer than You.
>
> – *Dr. Seuss*

Many people have developed a habit of connecting through life drama. There is a place for drama and it's more likely at the theater, not the center stage of your life. Much like alcohol or caffeine, is it possible you have gotten addicted to the buzz? With every juicy story comes another opportunity to stand on center stage and see if you can command an audience. Will they listen as you introduce them to the evil characters in your life, your role as the victim and the intriguing (to you) plot? Will your listeners give you sympathy and be willing to join your fight, give you a standing ovation as you take another bow, or maybe even ask for an encore—which you just happened to have conveniently prepared?

The challenge with that mode of living is that you're dependent on keeping the drama going. As you go through your day, you are replaying how you'll tell the story and get the reactions you'll need from your fan base. It takes you out of the present moment and into a future narrative. Eventually, people see you as a drama addict and you will either burn them out or you'll be surrounded by people who also have a high need for drama and dysfunction.

PRACTICE

Before you start to tell the next scintillating story of how your boss screwed you over or your family treated you like crap, stop and reflect by asking yourself:

1. Is what I'm about to share 100% true?
2. Is it uplifting and might it add value for the listener?
3. Have I told this story more than once or twice? If so, what is my motivation to repeat it?
4. What was my role in creating this drama?
5. What could I learn from it? Grow from it? Or choose to do differently next time?

What if you knew that everything about you is acceptable? Not only acceptable, but perfectly OK?

You don't need to change anything about yourself to be OK. You are the only one walking the planet at this time that is exactly like you—with your experience, your thoughts, heart and soul.

RULE #10
Do for Others

RULE BREAKER
*Learn to Say No
Without the Guilt and Excuses*

Do you feel annoyed by how much time you have left at the end of the day? You've done everything on your to-do list, exercised, worked a full day, and still have much of the day left? Me neither. Most of us complain about being too busy. Yet, when someone makes a request of us that requires a commitment of our time and energy, we quickly reply yes, I'll do it! It's like the reflex hammer—isn't it fun to keep doing it to see if your leg will jerk up as the hammer hits your knee? We have a reflex to say yes to requests without pausing to consider our needs and wants. How many times, right after saying "yes," have you slapped your forehead and thought: "Oh no! Why did I say yes to that? I'd rather have a root canal."

If you had given yourself a brief moment to think, you may not have said yes. Instead, you may have made a different decision about how and when to invest your time and energy.

A Simple Model to Help You Break the Yes Habit

There is value in having a system to break yourself of the 'yes' habit. There is one critical step that is usually missing from our process. Instead of going directly from hearing a request to responding to it, try this:

Hear the request from the other person. For example, Would you be willing to join this volunteer committee and help?

Step 1: ACKNOWLEDGE AND EMPATHIZE. We want the other person to feel heard and their request to be valued. Make a simple statement to reflect what you've heard: "It sounds as though you need some additional help for the committee and that it's important to you to find a quality person."

Step 2: GUT CHECK. This is the part we often skip over, which leads us to saying yes too quickly. Take a few seconds or minutes to check in with yourself and get a temperature read on how you feel about the request. Is it a resounding yes? Your initial feeling is—that sounds great! Or, is it an absolute NO, that request sounds awful and I'd rather have my molars torn out of my mouth. Or is it somewhere in between—hmm, it could have possibilities, I am not sure yet. If you are in person or on the phone, this gut check may be as quick as one deep breath while becoming aware of what you're feeling. If you're reading the request in an email or in a situation that is not as time sensitive, build in this step of pausing—whether that means stepping away from the computer, or sleeping on it until the next day.

STEP 3: ELIMINATE THE YES: Based on your first gut feeling, practice choosing a "no" or "maybe" response. Because we are aiming to break the "yes" habit and it is easy to have that as our default, we're temporarily eliminating it as an option. You can add it back in later once your "no" muscle is much stronger.

A request is made of you

Step 1

Acknowledge & Empathize

Step 2

Don't answer before you pause and do a . . .

Gut Check

Step 3

How do I feel?

No Way!   Sounds Interesting

NO   **MAYBE**

Step 4

"It's not a fit for me"
No Guilt or Excuses

Set a Time Frame
for Response

STEP 4: ASSIGN A TIME FRAME: When you respond with "maybe," give a time frame of when you'll get back to them so that they have a closed loop. Always give yourself more time than you think you'll need. Think you need an hour? Tell them you'll get back to them by end of business day. You want to sleep on it? Tell them you'll get back to them in three days.

STEP 5: AVOID THE APOLOGIES AND EXCUSES: If your gut check tells you there is absolutely no way you are interested, say no. Then, avoid a typical impulse to attach explanations to it. How many times do we find ourselves telling white lies about why we can't attend an event or help someone out? It is perfectly ok to say: Thanks for asking but right now, it's not a fit for me.

My son heard this process so many times that by the time he was a teenager, he'd say, "Mom, I need a new snowboard this season because I've outgrown mine. How much time do you need to get back to me on this?"

In addition to yourself, it's also a good skill to teach kids and employees. Their crisis is not your emergency. Most things can wait a few days—and it models delayed gratification. Remember that you are training people how to treat you. If you've trained people to know that you're the one to ask if they need a yes, because you'll always say yes and you don't set boundaries or take care of yourself—then take responsibility for your choices when you're overloaded.

If you're overloaded, practice breaking the yes habit and prioritizing those things that energize you.

It's easy to throw in guilt and excuses when we say no. In fact, even the most honest person has been caught lying when it comes to saying no to a request and feeling the need to make up a reason. Suddenly there is that fictional social obligation or a family trip to Alaska to get you out of the situation. Practice saying no without the guilt and excuses. Thank you for asking. It's not a fit for me at this time. There doesn't need to be a reason to say no. Is that mean? Well, it may feel that way when it is unfamiliar. But, couldn't it be considered equally "mean" to commit to something when you know you aren't going to have the time or energy for it and you'll end up doing it begrudgingly? What is the guilt about? Do you have a belief that you are only as valuable as what you produce? Are you worried about people not liking you if you set limits on what you're willing to do?

Is there someone you chronically complain about, who irritates you at work or socially that you need to be more direct in saying no to? Are you assuming that they shouldn't be asking you, when in fact, you have trained them to over-rely on you?

If you tend to be a "yes" person but have a victim mentality about it, you may have beliefs about why you can't say no. These are some typical examples:

- I have to pack my children's suitcases for them or they'll forget something important.
- I need to be on that committee again this year because I've always done it and they are counting on me.
- I have to cook for my family every night because my partner would just make mac and cheese for the kids and would leave the kitchen a mess.

Take time to answer these questions so that you gain a better understanding of your own habits:

- Who are you allowing to under-function so that you can continue to over-function?
- What would happen if you gave up over-functioning?
- What are you afraid might happen?
- What are the payoffs for you to stay in overachiever mode?
- Is it more important that things get done and taken off your plate, or is it more important to you that things get done your way?

Sometimes, we talk ourselves into saying yes because the opportunity dangles a carrot in front of us. Our gut is telling us no, but we argue that it could lead to something big. My brother shared a great story about his own experience with this. André is an incredible high school teacher; he is gifted in being able to communicate with teens and his students love him. At an earlier point in his career when he was doing private tutoring, he got a call from a celebrity artist of whom he was a huge fan. He was invited to tutor the celebrity's child at their home.

After rescheduling with him four times in five days, the private assistant arranged a 2:00 pm appointment for André to meet the celebrity's wife and talk about the tutoring. He arrived at their trendy 41st floor New York City apartment on time and learned that Mrs. Celebrity was running 20 or 30 minutes late. He was asked to go and hang out at a coffee shop until she returned, at which time he'd be summoned back by phone. Feeling annoyed as he walked to Starbucks, he decided to give them twenty minutes to call. Forty minutes later when the assistant called to say he could return, André said he wouldn't be able to meet and that upon reflection, he had to decline the tutoring position because it did not feel like a good match. The assistant was flustered and began justifying how hectic the mother's schedule had been, including having just received an award from the White House. She went on to assure André that he would be working directly with the son and his nanny and therefore wouldn't need to coordinate with the Mom's schedule. André held firm in trusting his instinct and declining the opportunity. To their credit, Mrs. Celebrity called him later and left a very gracious and apologetic message.

There were plenty of reasons that saying yes would have made sense. Being a massive fan of the celebrity's music and enamored with the idea of tutoring their kid, he also knew it could very easily lead to other celebrity gigs. He had not been tutoring long and did not yet have anywhere near a full schedule or much income. The stakes were highly slanted towards persevering and nevertheless, he valued his feeling that it wasn't going to be a good fit. Sometimes, it's tough to say no to something that may have tempting payoffs. Taking time for the "gut check" as André was able to do on his way to Starbucks, is one way to get clear on whether it is a yes or no.

What are you willing to try?

PRACTICE

Thoughts to consider for change:
- You may need to let go of things being done your way.
- You may need to let go of control.
- You may need to be tolerant and patient with what you view as mistakes.
- You may need to tolerate uncertainty and ambiguity during that transition from you doing it all to allowing others to pick up tasks and new skills.
- You may need to say no to something that others think you're crazy not to accept.

RULE #11
History Repeats Itself

RULE BREAKER
Change Your Story

Focusing on what we lack is the quickest route down the black hole. Focusing on lack tends to create a low-level energy, from apathy to depression to giving up. What you lack is often a clue to what you need to give away. Feeling lonely and in lack of love? Find a way to give love to someone who might be lonely. Feeling broke and focused on lack of money? Seek opportunities to share what you do have. Feeling frightened? Go comfort someone who is also afraid.

Every feeling passes. Nothing is permanent. Whether you're high on life or in the pits of despair, this feeling is going to pass fairly quickly. Many of our worst decisions are made in the moments we get tricked into thinking a feeling is permanent and we act from that moment. Feeling rage and lashing out. Feeling infatuated and making a commitment. Feeling depressed and attempting to take our life. When a storm blows in, you may close all the windows, or even take to the basement in a tornado and batten down the hatches, but eventually you look back out for signs it has passed and that it's safe to re-surface. The same is true for our feelings—we may need to batten down the hatches but we know that storms pass. Develop the habit of reminding yourself that this will pass.

This new practice will feel strange because for many, it is the exact opposite of what you're conditioned to do. What I'm proposing is that you move towards that which you have usually avoided. For example, if you feel lonely, you may be conditioned to hole up at home and think about how you wish you had more friends and social invitations. That habit of moving towards the loneliness and isolation has become comfortable for you and although it's not fun, and it doesn't make you feel better, you know how to do it. You sit at home and think, yes I'm so lonely. This is who and what I am.

It takes more energy to push yourself out the door the next time you feel lonely and force yourself to stop by a friend's house or go help at a volunteer project. It requires you to fight the gravitational pull of the familiar old habits that have gotten you to this point. Every part of you might be screaming that you just want to be left alone and that you don't have the energy. It's a big and important choice each time you decide whether you'll do the same old familiar thing or break your former rules about how you live and instead, do the opposite of the way you've always done it.

Learn from your Past

There may be things from the past that you're unknowingly giving too much weight to. The past does not equal the future. The past can be generalized to create biases. You had a bad experience with someone driving like an idiot in Minneapolis and now you believe that people in Minneapolis are terrible drivers. In the past, you've made poor choices in relationships, so now you are convinced that you're bad with relationships.

Carry the past more lightly. Instead of it being a ten pound brick in your backpack, maybe it's more like a snack bar and half an apple.

Avoiding pain is one of our driving forces. We remember most of our painful moments from the past. Turn your back on your past. Spend most of your time standing firmly grounded in your present with your eyes and heart ahead to the future.

Our cells reproduce at a rate that results in our physical bodies being completely renewed and changed every eight years. Therefore, we are not even the same person physically that we were in the past! Ponder that.

People often have reasons they can't change. Reasons their life can't be better.

I'm fat because it runs in my family.

My dad was an entrepreneur and went bankrupt so I could never start my own business.

I was abused as a child so I don't trust people.

It's easy to hang on to these reasons and to stay stuck.

Do Whatever You Want With Your Life but Take 100% Personal Responsibility

You're not fat because of your family genes. You're fat because you eat more than you burn off. You're not broke because of the economy. You're broke because you haven't learned how to save more money than you spend. The past can make you believe that something is too risky or even impossible. It may have been, in the past, but it does not necessarily hold true for the present or future.

I felt physically awkward and self-conscious while growing up. I was tall and lanky but had no confidence to play high school sports and chose to sit out on the sidelines. Then, I moved to Colorado after college where almost everyone is active. Insanely active. Running up mountains, ultra-marathons, climbing 14,000 foot peaks active. I learned to ski again for the first time since breaking my leg while skiing when I was eight years old. I ran my first marathon when I turned fifty-one, never having previously been a "runner," and I've become more active each year. Don't let the past define you. I had to push through my old story about being clumsy and having no athletic skills to creating an open mind about what was possible for me.

We all have our stories and then look for evidence that validates those stories. We get attached to our stories to the point where we can't tell fact from fiction. What if we put less energy into supporting them and more energy into proving why they're wrong?

Memory is anchored in strong emotion. If I asked you to tell me what it was like when you were fifteen years old, you are unlikely to recall the entire year. But, you will remember vignettes, generally that were high emotions: losses, loves, heartbreak, highs. In remembering those key highly charged moments, we forget about all the other more mundane times. Those not so memorable moments could offer a richer tapestry for our story. For example, in my own story, there probably were times when I was involved in athletics—I can remember skating on the nearby ice rink in Minnesota's subzero temperatures and playing softball after dinner with all the neighborhood kids in the warmer months.

When you rely on the past for learning, ask yourself: "Am I sure this is true for me NOW?" And if the answer comes back saying yes, it is still true, then I encourage you to test that. Take some action numerous times to see if you can prove yourself wrong. You have a story that you're a terrible cook (but secretly you've always wished you were good)? Partner up with a friend who is an excellent cook and have them walk you through the steps from A to Z to creating a successful recipe. Start spinning a different story. Consider changing the language you use to describe yourself. You could transition to saying: "I used to not be comfortable cooking and now I'm learning to enjoy it and I can make a few dishes that are delicious." Be willing to see yourself with new skills, new strengths, and new opportunities rather than deciding that the way you have been in the past will be the way you are in the future.

PRACTICE

What are some limiting things I often say about myself?

_____

_____

_____

_____

Am I open to changing that story?

_____

_____

_____

What could my new story line be?

_____

_____

_____

What action can I take to support my new story?

_____

_____

_____

_____

RULE #12
Death is a Tragedy

RULE BREAKER
No One Gets Out of Here Alive

More than a decade ago, my husband passed away after a five-month battle with kidney cancer. On reflection, there are so many lessons I learned, a few of which I'd like to share with you.

When Garry was diagnosed with Stage IV cancer, I hadn't personally known anyone with cancer and the only funeral I had been to was my ninety-three-year-old grandmother's. To say I was inexperienced with death is an understatement. Fortunately, I was surrounded by an amazing group of friends and family who created a safety net for my son, Tanner, and me, ensuring that we would be loved and supported every step of the way. I share these thoughts in the hope that they might be helpful to you or someone you know and to invite you to think about (rather than avoid) the inevitable topic of death.

For most of my adult life I prided myself on being independent, and avoided asking others for help. Can any of you relate to that? Whether it was moving furniture on my own, or hosting a dinner party where I handled all the work, I liked the feeling of being self-sufficient. During Garry's illness, I could no longer do it all myself. After his first emergency surgery, my sister-in-law looked me straight in the eyes and said, "You're going to need to let people help you." Although I was initially surprised by her comment, she was absolutely right. As the months progressed, it was impossible to be at Garry's doctor appointments and pick Tanner up from school at the same time. It was impossible to be up at the emergency room all night and be functional for work the next day. I began to say "yes" to friends who offered to do things for me. I said "yes" more often than it felt comfortable. I learned that other people genuinely wanted to do something, it was not a burden for them. I was forced to do a whole lot less every day and learned not to judge my day by my productivity.

When we know someone who is in a crisis, it's natural to say, "Let me know if I can do anything." While well-intentioned, it's highly unlikely that the person in need will ask. They are busy trying to keep their head above water and are not going to have the energy to reach out. Instead, offer to do something specific and make it easy for them to say yes. For example, in the fall season you could say: "We're busy raking leaves at our house today and the kids have so much energy. Would it be helpful if we stop by and rake your leaves too?" Avoid taking it personally if they decline your offer and try to offer another kind of help again some other day.

If, like me, you are a person who has always done it yourself, don't wait for a major life event to break that habit. The next time someone offers to help, say yes even though it is uncomfortable. You don't have to need the help in order to accept the help. It's not a sign of weakness or being incapable. Yes, you know you could handle it yourself—but how about allowing space for human connection and vulnerability? You acting as though you don't need anyone else, serves no one.

Another important lesson came in realizing I had mistakenly thought "hospice" meant someone was a few days from death. What I learned is that hospice is a philosophy, not a place or time frame. A family can call them any time after a diagnosis of a terminal illness and use their services for up to six or more months. The hospice staff is indescribably at ease with death and dying. Unlike most of us, and most of the medical system, they are not shy about giving an opinion as to how long a person has to live, giving a patient as many meds as they need to be comfortable, and engaging family members in tough conversations. They even had a harp player come to Garry's room at hospice and give us the most beautiful private performance shortly before Garry passed away. As I sat at Garry's beside bobbing for apples from pure exhaustion, hospice staff came in and told me that I should wake up and be alert because he would be dying within the next 30 minutes. Isn't that crazy that first of all, they know that, and secondly they are kind enough to say it? It gave me the opportunity to be awake with Garry as he took his last breath. I can't say it enough: if you have a family member at any stage of a terminal illness, call hospice and talk to them about your situation today. Hospice can be at your home or at one of their facilities—you have choices.

Many of us grew up learning about Elisabeth Kübler-Ross's model of grief, which includes the five stages of denial, anger, bargaining, depression, and acceptance. Although I would guess it was included in her body of work, I missed the part about the stages not being linear or predictable. I thought a person went through them neatly, one at a time, and then moved on to the next one. Instead, what I learned is that the stages are fluid, often repeating themselves and not in any logical way. I could have a calm day of acceptance interrupted by a storm of anger that threatened to swallow me like a riptide with no warning. Hearing a certain song or seeing someone who looked like Garry might send me into a crying jag at the most inopportune moments. If you are grieving, be gentle with yourself about the process—it can be a crazy ride! If you know someone who is grieving, don't assume they are in the same state from one day to the next. Leave room for them to tell you how they are doing rather than make assumptions.

I learned that it is exceedingly difficult to know what a loved one wants while they are seriously ill. A person in extreme pain is unlikely to be able to communicate what they need. You may think they'd like you keeping them company in bed when what they really want is to be left alone. You may assume they want organic vegetables when, in fact, it makes them happiest to eat lemon meringue pie and drink soda (it took a scolding nurse for me to finally get the message that Garry didn't want another one of my organic green smoothies and to stop being such a control freak with his diet. At that point in his illness, it wasn't going to make a difference!). Take a look at The Five Wishes and consider completing them with your family, while everyone is healthy and it is easier to have the discussion. It facilitates the conversation about each family member's personal preferences. www.aging-withdignity.org

I learned that a deathbed scene is not necessarily like a Hollywood movie where all the loved ones are standing around having deep conversations and heartfelt goodbyes. Garry didn't say anything for many days before leaving and there were no coherent goodbyes. While I was glad to be with him for his last breaths, there was much left unsaid, and I imagine there often is. People who are dying are not always filled with love and wisdom. Garry was pissed off that he was dying, and he was a demanding patient. All of that is part of losing a love—it can be messy. Strangely, there was also an element of surprise—no matter how much you might prepare for someone's death, it can still feel surprising when it happens. It did for me. When you are talking with someone who just experienced the death of a loved one, rather than saying "Oh, it must be so hard" or "I'm sorry that they went before their time", which are your personal perspectives, try listening to them to understand what they are experiencing—it may be different than you think.

On a very practical level, I learned that extreme back pain just below the ribs, particularly for men in their fifties, is a symptom of kidney cancer and should serve as a red flag for further examination. Initially, we thought that Garry's recent beginner snowboarding lessons, which included plenty of wipe-outs, were the explanation for his back pain. Our chiropractor was the first one to voice concern that the pain was something more serious. Keep this is mind if you hear of men dealing with back pain that doesn't go away.

I've learned that love and time really do heal; that's not just corny sentiment. Our hearts are incredibly resilient and it is human nature to find a way to get back up and keep moving forward. I learned that it is much easier to do that surrounded by people who love us, of whom there are many, if we allow them in. And I've learned that our losses and heartache shape the person we become: we can choose to be a person filled with bitterness and anger, or we can choose to allow our losses to soften our edges.

We spend so much time in life worrying and wondering what other people will think about our choices and our life. In the end, it stunned me to realize how very alone we are as we take our final bow. It is completely up to each of us to create a life that we feel good about, regardless of what anyone else has to say about it.

Conclusion

You are the expert on your own life. This book offers you ways to begin taking steps in the direction you want to go. I hope that you will be willing to try some new things and give yourself credit for being the one "in the know" about your wants, needs, and goals.

Make a daily practice to look within for knowledge and direction rather than bending to every external pressure that comes your way. People will disagree with you, challenges will occur. Friends and family may put subtle (or not so subtle!) pressure on you to try and get you to be the way you've always been because it makes their life easier. The more you can develop an internal compass, the less you'll feel thrown around by the inevitable winds.

Change can be messy in that we don't necessarily see immediate results. In fact, often times things appear to be temporarily worse before they are better. Stay the course. Surround yourself with people who believe in you and your ability to create a life that you love. Be gentle with yourself during the practice of new habits and remind yourself that you've done things the same way for years—it makes sense that it feels awkward to do it differently.

Let me know how you're doing and how I can support your growth and change. My favorite part about doing the work that I do, is connecting with you. Really! I'd love to hear from you personally about what's been valuable to you in reading this, what's working in your life as well as what challenges you are having. Let's continue the conversation. I welcome your email at sylvia@sylviatheisen.com.

Favorite Resources

Earlier in this book, I mentioned that a common complaint from readers of personal development books seems to be "Meh — nothing new." As discussed, I have a different opinion about that because I don't believe there is a new magical 'one thing' that is going to completely change my life. I've used dozens of tools over the years that have each helped me in different ways, adding to my growth and positive direction. If I gain one new idea, develop one new habit or shift an old belief, I consider that to have been valuable. Building an ever-growing tool box of things that help me to feel more positive, more motivated, more peaceful is something that I value as a life-long practice. At different times in my life, different things have been the most useful. As an alternative to seeking one thing, I invite you to create your own combination of helpful resources. Here are some of my favorites:

BOOKS (in no particular order)

The Big Magic, by Elizabeth Gilbert
I love the inspiration this book offers about our relationship to our creativity. Reading it helped me to feel more free about writing, speaking and creatively expressing myself.

The Compound Effect, by Darren Hardy
A practical look at how small habits and changes can make a huge difference. Darren Hardy also has a 'Darren Daily' program — which you can receive via email or text. You'll receive short daily videos for motivation and inspiration in business and in life.

You are a Badass, *by Jen Sincero*

Jen Sincero is funny and real. She shares the less- than-stellar phases of her life and how she changed the quality of her life by making bold decisions, being persistent and improving her mindset. She does use a lot of cursing and has an irreverent style — so if that offends you, I wouldn't choose this one. Her latest book is You are a Badass with Money, which I have not yet read.

You Can Heal Your Life, *by Louise Hay*

An old classic, this was one of the first book I read decades ago that opened my eyes to how our thoughts and beliefs impact the external outcomes.

Creative Visualization, *by Shatki Gwain*

Another classic; a simple and easy read. Filled with examples on how to use our subconscious mind and visualization to more easily move towards goals and manifest in our lives.

The Success Principles, *by Jack Canfield*

This isn't a book I would ever read from beginning to end, but I enjoy picking it up for an occasional positive reading — often just one chapter at a time.

The Big Leap, *by Gay Hendricks*

This book started so slowly that I almost didn't continue reading it, but I'm glad I did. The concept about self-sabotaging when we reach our "upper limit" as well as the chapters on our zones of competence were really worthwhile and have stuck with me.

Ask and It is Given, by Esther and Jerry Hicks.
This book is a staple for those who follow Abraham Hicks. I don't understand a whole lot about channeling and am always a bit skeptical, but not sure it matters. What I do know is that I feel better when I practice these techniques and when I listen to Abraham Hicks audios. There must be something to the theory of raising your vibrational level because I feel that when I follow these practices. If you're not in to the 'woo woo' factor, pass on it. It's definitely not for everyone.

You 2, by Price Pritchett
it's easy to overlook this book because it's so short (35 pages) but packed with profound insights. Unconventional strategies about taking a big leap forward with less effort rather than struggling through small incremental steps. If you're in need of a boost and are open to quantum physics, I think you'll like it.

Prince Charming Isn't Coming, by Barbara Stanny
A good book for any woman (because it is particularly for female readers) wanting to better understand her relationship with money. The author is the daughter of one of the founders of H&R Block and went through her own journey of not understanding or trusting herself to handle her finances, before she went on to teach others.

The Art of Money, by Barri Tessler
If you want to take a deep dive into the psychological aspects of dealing with money, this is a good one. Just FYI - It includes topics of spirituality and self-care, so it's different than a Dave Ramsey style of how to budget. Equally applicable to men and women.

ON BUILDING A BUSINESS:

Mark LeBlanc – A business coach based out of Minneapolis, MN. Mark has written a classic book called Growing Your Business and is an expert on small business, Mark offers weekend workshops called Achievers Circle as well as individual coaching. He is an excellent coach and delivers from a place of genuinely wanting to help; he's not selling anything that isn't valuable.

Christine Kane – I've followed Christine for a long time and find her to be very down to earth and knowledgeable as a coach for independent business owners. She has a variety of online and 'live' programs.

Marie Forleo – a well-known online personality and business coach, I love her communication style and funny videos.

Brendon Burchard – International author, speaker, coach. Brendon is an enthusiastic personality and motivational guru for both personal and business life. He has hundreds of free YouTube videos as well as books, courses and live events. His book "The Charge" is a good one. There are habits I adopted from reading that book (i.e. "controlling for new") that have become part of my weekly habits and they are effective.

MISCELLANEOUS:

TUT "Thoughts Become Things" From their website – "Our mission is to remind others of life's fundamental truths: that life is magical, we are powerful, and dreams really do come true." You can sign up for daily playful messages from the Universe – short reads that land in your inbox in the morning. Always uplifting and funny, personalized with your name. I haven't participated in them, but they do also have live events.

EFT, Emotional Freedom Techniques, (Also called "tapping") – I don't understand how this can work, but it does for me. Tapping is a very simple technique that you can learn in minutes and do on yourself. Basically, you learn to tap your fingers at meridians on your face and upper body that are like acupuncture. If you tend to be scientifically based, you are likely to think it is nuts and throw it out, but if you're open to it – try it and decide for yourself. My favorite is Brad Yates on YouTube. He keeps it real, short and has a good sense of humor. I find it especially useful when I'm experiencing high anxiety or worry about something – a few rounds of "tapping" quickly decreases it.

Audible app – I'm listening to a lot more books now and this is a super easy and affordable app.

MyFitnessPal – a fun app for tracking your nutrition and exercise. You can also connect and support friends on it.

Meditation – Although I learned to do traditional TM style meditation many years ago with a breath mantra, sometimes I prefer to listen to guided meditations. There are several good apps, including one called "Insight Timer" that offers thousands of mediations with options to choose the theme, length and see the reviews. I use it when I am having difficulty sleeping – there are meditations particularly for going back to sleep that work well.

Carl Harvey / Abundance TV – If you're looking for some fresh motivation, check out Carl Harvey online. Among motivational gurus, he's a younger generation and he certainly does it in his own style – sitting in a hoodie and jeans in his office and talking openly. I like him and think he's funny. He has a book club called Abundance Book Club where members are sent a book

+ a gift a month and can then listen to webinars explaining the principles of the book.

I'm interested in learning about books, videos and tools that I may not have come across. Please share your favorites by emailing me at Sylvia@SylviaTheisen.com or join my Facebook community at https://www.facebook.com/SylviaTheisenSpeaker/. I look forward to hearing from you!

In Gratitude

To Tanner, I have learned so much from watching you trust your gut and create your own path in life regardless of what other people are doing. I love you mucho and know I am the luckiest Mom on the planet.

My parents, Vera and Sy—I'm forever grateful for the way you raised us in an environment of adventure and possibility. Thank you for the positive modeling, all the travel and cultural experiences and for your endless spirit of optimism.

To Caitlyn, Ben and Lowell, thank you for welcoming me into your world and accepting me fully, despite me having broken all the rules. You are each an unexpected gift in my world.

Huge thank you and hugs to André and Ann, and Julia—for being willing to read and re-read the draft and help me to get it to the finish line! I'm fortunate to have you as family and even luckier to know you as friends.

Thank you to my incredible group of amazing friends and a special shout out to Eddie. Thank you for valuing my words, advice and perspective; and encouraging me to share it all with others, for believing in me, and for embracing the whole concept of authenticity. Our friendship is a crazy good gift in my life.

To Richard Bryan and Angela Gaffney, as well as many more of my NSA CO friends—for your encouragement, friendship, sharing of resources and laughter along the way. It's so much more fun with your influence in my life.

To the amazing editor, Alexandra O'Connell who took my original scribbled notes and saw more in it than I did at the time; to the talented book cover designer and my friend, Paul

Vorreiter and Michelle White, for all your help. To Caitlin Johnson, without whom there never would have been a single blog post. Thank you to each of you for your patience and support along the way.

Massive appreciation to my supporters: those who have engaged with my blog, shared their experiences, connected at my live presentations and each of you who are holding this book. I look forward to continuing the conversations and creating a like-minded community through which we can all have a voice and learn from each other.

With Love,

Sylvia

About the Author

Sylvia Theisen knew from an early age that she would make a terrible employee because she likes to break the rules, is allergic to long meetings discussing minutia, and generally thinks she's the boss. Fortunately, decades of being a business owner worked out for her and she continues to love the entrepreneurial life despite its ups and downs.

After earning her Master's Degree in Clinical Social Work from the University of Denver, Sylvia's first career was as a psychotherapist—serving individuals, families, and corporate America. She later decided to close the doors on her private practice and dive into the world of sales where she earned the Hall of Fame Award from RE/MAX, LLC for her sales production.

Today, Sylvia runs a speaking and training business based in Denver, Colorado. Combining her love of psychology with her business acumen, she creates and delivers programs for companies, organizations, and associations. She is a regular contributor to the Huffington Post.

For more information about Sylvia's work or to book her to speak, please visit www.SylviaTheisen.com. She'd love to hear from you and your reviews of the book too at Sylvia@SylviaTheisen.com